Cambridge Elements ≡

Elements in Metaphysics
edited by
Tuomas E. Tahko
University of Bristol

MATERIAL OBJECTS

Thomas Sattig
University of Tübingen

CAMBRIDGE
UNIVERSITY PRESS

University Printing House, Cambridge CB2 8BS, United Kingdom

One Liberty Plaza, 20th Floor, New York, NY 10006, USA

477 Williamstown Road, Port Melbourne, VIC 3207, Australia

314–321, 3rd Floor, Plot 3, Splendor Forum, Jasola District Centre, New Delhi – 110025, India

103 Penang Road, #05–06/07, Visioncrest Commercial, Singapore 238467

Cambridge University Press is part of the University of Cambridge.

It furthers the University's mission by disseminating knowledge in the pursuit of education, learning, and research at the highest international levels of excellence.

www.cambridge.org
Information on this title: www.cambridge.org/9781009011464
DOI: 10.1017/9781009019606

First published 2021

A catalogue record for this publication is available from the British Library.

ISBN 978-1-009-01146-4 Paperback
ISSN 2633-9862 (online)
ISSN 2633-9854 (print)

Material Objects

Elements in Metaphysics

DOI: 10.1017/9781009019606
First published online: November 2021

Thomas Sattig
University of Tübingen

Author for correspondence: Thomas Sattig, thomas.sattig@uni-tuebingen.de

Abstract: This Element is a survey of central topics in the metaphysics of material objects. The topics are grouped into four problem spaces. The first concerns how an object's parts are related to the object's existence and to the object's nature or essence. The second concerns how an object persists through time, how an object is located in spacetime, and how an object changes. The third concerns paradoxes about objects, including paradoxes of coincidence, paradoxes of fission, and the problem of the many. The fourth concerns views with radical consequences regarding the existence of composite material objects, including mereological nihilism, ontological anti-realism, and deflationism..

Keywords: material objects, mereology, persistence, change, essence

ISBNs: 9781009011464 (PB), 9781009019606 (OC)
ISSNs: 2633-9862 (online), 2633-9854 (print)

Contents

Overview

This Element is a survey of central topics in the metaphysics of material objects. Section 1 is about metaphysical issues concerning material objects and their parts. The first issue is the special composition question, which concerns the conditions under which composite material objects exist. The second issue is whether material objects are structured or unstructured, which concerns the relationship between an object's parts and its nature or essence.

Section 2 is about metaphysical issues concerning the temporal profile of material objects. The section begins with the formulation of two metaphysical questions about the persistence of objects and the formulation of a range of answers to these questions. Subsequently, these answers are discussed in connection with various considerations about change.

Section 3 is about a range of paradoxes concerning material objects. A philosophical paradox marks the incompatibility of several pre-philosophically innocuous assumptions. The paradoxes of coincidence, the paradoxes of fission, and the problem of the many bring to the fore apparent inconsistencies in the manifest image of objects.

Section 4 is about radical departures from standard assumptions concerning the existence of composite material objects. The section begins with different considerations in support of mereological nihilism. Subsequently, the debate about the existence of composite material objects from Section 1 is reconceptualized from the point of view of alternatives to standard ontological realism.

1 Parts

Our tour of the metaphysics of material objects will begin with two metaphysical issues concerning material objects and their parts. The first issue, to be discussed in Sections 1.1 and 1.2, concerns the relationship between an object's parts and its existence. The second issue, to be discussed in Section 1.3, concerns the relationship between an object's parts and its nature or essence.

1.1 Composition and Existence

A central problem in contemporary metaphysics concerns the links between the existence of a material object and its parts. Consider any plurality of objects – let us call them 'the xs'. Under what conditions does an object that is composed of the xs exist? This is widely known as the *special composition question* (SCQ) (van Inwagen, 1990, sect. 2). An answer to SCQ specifies when composition occurs.

It is now standard to classify possible answers to SCQ as follows. First, according to *restrictivist* answers to SCQ, the *x*s must have some non-trivial property or stand in some non-trivial relation in order to compose something. If composition is restricted, then it is sometimes true and sometimes false that some *x*s compose something. Different specifications of non-trivial principles of composition are grouped under the label *mereological restrictivism* (van Inwagen, 1990). Second, *mereological universalism* (Lewis, 1986) is an alternative answer to SCQ, which places no restrictions on what the *x*s must be like in order for them to compose something. The mere existence of the *x*s is necessary and sufficient for the existence of an object composed of the *x*s. As a consequence, composition occurs always. Third, according to *mereological nihilism* (Sider, 2013) there are no composite objects at all. This is less a solution to the problem of when composition occurs than a dissolution of the problem. Since composition never occurs, the task of specifying when it occurs just disappears.

How should we decide among mereological restrictivism, universalism, and nihilism? Three strategies of evaluating answers to SCQ can be distinguished. The first strategy is to approach SCQ under the auspices of the *manifest image of objects*. The manifest image, or the common-sense conception, comprises pre-theoretical beliefs and intuitions about the world that most of us share. The manifest image of objects clearly features composites. They are the objects with which we intentionally interact, the objects that furnish our everyday lives, often called 'ordinary objects'. They have smaller objects as parts. Organisms, like us, have organs as parts. Trees have branches as parts. Pianos have strings as parts. There is a substantive meta-philosophical debate about whether in doing metaphysics the manifest image should be consulted at all. Those who take it seriously place significant weight on match with common sense when evaluating answers to SCQ. In this methodological setting, our intuitive existence judgements about objects are viewed as providing a guide for answering SCQ. SCQ is thus seen as raising the challenge of linking composition with existence in a way that best matches our pre-theoretical judgements about which material objects exist and which do not exist.

Let us look at an example. On a table, illustrated in Figure 1, we find a metal blade, a wooden handle – physically connected in the way illustrated – and a potato. Pretend, for simplicity, that the mentioned objects lack any parts. How many objects are to be found on the table? Intuitively, there are four objects on the table: the blade, the handle, a knife composed of the blade and the handle, and the potato. So the only composite object that exists in this scenario is the knife. There are no others. The blade and the potato do not compose a further object. Nor do the handle and the potato. Nor do the blade and the handle, and the potato. Why so?

Figure 1 Composition in the kitchen

A prima facie plausible answer, which captures these ordinary judgements about which composite objects exist, is that for a plurality of objects, the *x*s, to compose a further object, the *x*s must stand in some non-trivial physical relation. Since, in our case, only the blade and the handle are physically connected, they compose a further object, namely, the knife. This is a restrictivist answer to SCQ. Mereological restrictivism is the natural position when SCQ is answered by recourse to the manifest image. According to mereological universalism, by contrast, there are four composites on the table and not just the knife. There is also the whole composed of the blade and the potato, the whole composed of the handle and the potato, and the whole composed of the knife and the potato. By the lights of common sense, universalism is inferior to restrictivism because universalism recognizes too many objects, while restrictivism gets the intuitive number of objects right. Finally, according to mereological nihilism, there are no composite material objects at all. Pretending that the handle, the blade, and the potato have no parts, we find there are only these three objects on the table. There is no knife on the table since no mereological simples ever compose anything. In light of the manifest image, nihilism is the most radical take on SCQ. If nihilism is correct, then vast portions of our ordinary conception of the world are misguided.[1]

The second strategy is to evaluate answers to SCQ in the context of a general, topic-neutral theory of parthood relations, a theory in the field of *mereology*.[2] The aim of such a theory is to specify general principles governing the

---

[1] While mereological nihilists are *eliminativists* about ordinary objects, not all eliminativists about ordinary objects are mereological nihilists (Unger, 1979; van Inwagen, 1990).

[2] For an overview of the current state of the art, see Cotnoir & Varzi, 2021.

relationships between a whole and its parts. Mereology is frequently compared to set theory, whose aim is to specify general principles governing the relationship between a set and its members. SCQ is just one among many challenges that such a theory faces. Moreover, material objects are not the only examples of wholes to which SCQ applies, and hence there are further cases that a general theory of parts aims to subsume. Other examples are quantities, events, processes, facts, propositions, and sentences. While mereologists may well pay attention to the pre-theoretical verdicts of common sense, their methodological outlook exerts no pressure to treat the vindication of the manifest image of objects as a weighty desideratum in theory-building. It is no surprise, then, that in contemporary mereology, restrictivism does not typically have the status of being a more promising starting point than universalism. No serious mereologist will flirt with full-blown mereological nihilism, though, as the latter makes mereology obsolete.

The third strategy is to evaluate answers to SCQ by recourse to scientific theories, in particular to theories in physics. Most metaphysicians agree that the compatibility of their ideas with our best theories in physics is an important requirement. Many hold, furthermore, that if physics has something to say about which composite material objects exist, and about which principles of composition are best suited to underwrite the existence of these composites, then the pronouncements of physics are to be given greater weight in theorizing than those of common sense. Since apparently physics is concerned with material composites, such as physical molecules, one cannot be blamed for pleading that SCQ belongs on the desk of physicists or at least that of philosophers of physics. We must tread with caution, though. While it is easy to accept that in a direct conflict between physics and the manifest image, physics wins any day, what follows from this for answering SCQ is more complicated than it might appear at first. For it is highly controversial whether material objects play an indispensable role in our best theories of physics. The notion of a composite object, as it appears in physics, might just be a convenient import from the manifest image, without bearing any real weight in physical theories (Rosen & Dorr, 2002). It cannot simply be taken for granted that physics is an arbiter in the metaphysics of objects. Whether physics has a say is a substantive matter – such is the case for other branches of science featuring composite material objects.

The ambitious metaphysician takes all three strategies into consideration. In the confines of this Element, a more focused approach is called for. And so the discussion of SCQ in Section 1.2 will be framed by the first strategy, which has been central in discussions of SCQ of the last thirty years. Since anyone guided by the manifest image accepts that there are composite material objects, mereological restrictivism and universalism will be the protagonists in what follows, while mereological nihilism will be set aside until later. A discussion of SCQ following the demanding second strategy, which reaches far beyond the domain of material objects, will not be attempted here. But the comparatively young attempt to 'naturalize' the study of material composites, manifested in the third strategy, will be taken up in Section 4.1, in which mereological nihilism will resurface.

1.2 Mereological Restrictivism and Universalism

By the lights of common sense, mereological restrictivism is the most promising answer to SCQ. The approach faces major objections, though. I shall look at two of them.

1.2.1 The Specification Objection

Most restrictivists assume that there is a unique relation, R, that governs composition across the domain of material objects: necessarily, for any xs, there is an object composed of the xs iff the xs stand in R. There is, further, a widespread expectation that R is intelligible. It should elicit no applause to announce that composition is restricted while we cannot understand how it is restricted. So what is R? Given that restrictivists approach SCQ under the auspices of the manifest image of objects, they face the challenge of specifying R in a way that captures our pre-theoretical judgements about which material objects exist and which do not exist. As it turns out, this is an exceedingly difficult task.

As a first attempt, one might propose to understand composition as restricted by the topological relation of *contact*: necessarily, for any xs, there is an object composed of the xs iff the xs are in contact with one another (van Inwagen, 1990, sect. 3). In our case, intuition passes the verdict that there is a composite object, the knife, composed of the blade and the handle. The contact principle requires the blade and the handle to be in contact, which they seem to be. But now look at the knife under a microscope. Many more parts of the knife than the blade and the handle are thus revealed. While the knife is composed of physical particles such as electrons, these microscopic objects cannot be described as being in contact. So the contact principle has straightforward counterexamples.

As a second attempt, one might seek to understand composition as restricted by a physical relation that makes a plurality of objects stick together somehow: necessarily, for any xs, there is an object composed of the xs iff the xs are *fastened* together (van Inwagen, 1990, p. 56). This is really just an under-specified schema that is to be replaced ultimately by a scientifically more informed principle. But let us work with what we've got. The fastenation principle takes care of the knife's microscopic parts as these are, intuitively, fastened together. But the principle fails to capture other cases. Imagine a modular housing project in which each house is composed, inter alia, of walls that are not fastened to each other but are rather fastened to walls of other houses, as illustrated in Figure 2. Suppose, further, that these walls stand on wheels, for quick rearrangement, and hence that they are not fastened to the floor. So the walls are not related by the transitive closure of fastenation. Imagine, finally, that the four walls of each house do not even touch, leaving narrow gaps. This is a counterexample to both the fastenation principle and the contact principle of composition.

A house of this sort is a full-blown composite material object, which the two principles fail to cover. Intuitively, the arrangement of parts that underlies composition in this case is a functional arrangement that requires neither physical bonding nor physical contact among any of the composite's parts. Since the parts of the knife can also be seen as unified by a certain functional arrangement, one might pursue restrictivism with the aim of formulating a function-based principle of composition. But which function-based principle should we take to govern composition? There are so many different suitable candidates. What has the functional arrangement of a knife's parts to do with the functional arrangement of a house's parts or with that of an organism's parts? Furthermore, what makes a function suitable to govern composition? The function of two-way communication is served by a pair of two-way radios, where one is located on the Earth and the other is located in a space capsule

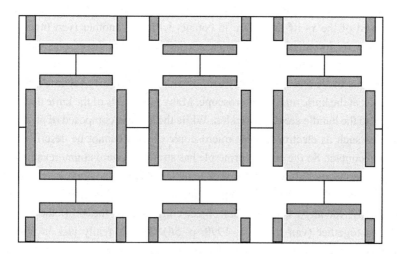

Figure 2 Composition without fastenation

orbiting the Earth.[3] Since the two radios arguably fail to compose anything, the function of two-way communication is not suitable to govern composition. Finally, what is the functional arrangement of the parts of a rock? In the latter case, it makes more sense to hold that composition is triggered by some sort of physical bonding.[4]

Consideration of a few simple cases such as these is enough to get the impression that the project of specifying a principle of composition that achieves a perfect fit with folk ontology is hopeless. This is the specification objection to mereological restrictivism. What to do? In response, one might be inclined to loosen the requirement that the principle of composition should yield a perfect fit with the manifest image. Perhaps it will do to formulate a principle of composition that captures only some of our ordinary existence claims about objects. But which ordinary objects do we want to save? It is hard to give a non-arbitrary answer.

Perhaps, then, it is time to remove the discussion of SCQ from the grip of common-sense philosophers, and to hand the problem over to physicists, chemists, or biologists, in order for them to provide empirical support for one composition principle over its rivals and thereby to teach us which ordinary objects to accept as real. As pointed out in Section 1.1, this move amounts to switching strategies of evaluating SCQ – it is a switch from the first to the third strategy mentioned there. Moreover, as I also pointed out, there are reasons to hold that facts about which composite objects are mentioned by successful scientific theories should not be assigned much weight in the debate about SCQ.[5]

1.2.2 The Indeterminacy Objection

A second widely discussed objection to mereological restrictivism concerns *indeterminacy*.[6] The objection is that restrictivism is committed to a disturbing form of indeterminacy. Suppose that we settle on the fastenation version of restrictivism (setting aside counterexamples). Consider a continuous series of cases running from the beginning to the end of the assembly of the knife of Section 1.1 (cf. Korman, 2010, p. 891). This is known as a *sorites series*. In the first case, the handle and the blade are not fastened together and hence do not

---

[3] This example is due to Hestevold (1981, p. 374).

[4] For discussion of the role of functions in the manifest image of composition, see Korman & Carmichael, 2017 and Rose & Schaffer, 2017.

[5] For further discussion of the specification challenge, see Carmichael, 2015 and Markosian, 2008.

[6] See Lewis, 1986, pp. 212–13, and Sider, 2001, pp. 120–32. Some use the terms 'indeterminacy' and 'vagueness' interchangeably, others do not. In order to avoid confusion, I shall not speak of vagueness at all.

compose anything. In the last case, the handle and the blade are fastened together tightly and hence do compose something, namely, the knife. Furthermore, there are intermediate cases in the assembly series, in which the handle and the blade are fastened together less tightly than in the final case. Fastenation comes in degrees. At which degree of fastenation does composition begin? Where, in our series of cases in which the degree of fastenation increases in tiny steps, does the cut-off point for composition lie? Since the cases differ only minutely with respect to fastenation, placing the cut-off at any precise degree seems arbitrary. If, however, there is no precise degree of fastenation at which composition begins, then there are degrees of fastenation at which it is indeterminate whether composition occurs. There is a grey area of composition.

Case I in Figure 3 represents a case of determinate non-composition, case III represents a case of determinate composition, and case II represents a situation in which composition neither clearly occurs nor clearly fails to occur and hence represents a case of indeterminate composition.

This result has been viewed as disconcerting. Why so? There is no point battling indeterminacy. It is everywhere. For some people it is indeterminate whether they are tall. For some colour patches it is indeterminate whether they are red. But these cases of indeterminacy are harmless, from a metaphysical point of view, since they are cases of *representational indeterminacy*. In ordinary usage of

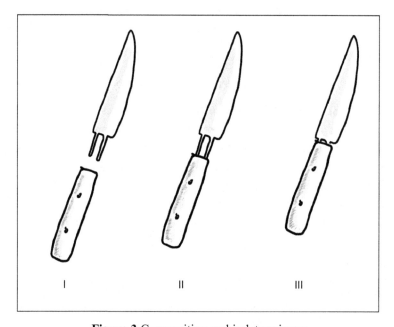

Figure 3 Composition and indeterminacy

the term 'tall' we never settled on a precise cut-off height at which the term begins to apply – likewise for the term 'red'. There is nothing particularly unsettling about this situation. When indeterminacy emerges from restricted composition, by contrast, the world starts to crumble. By the fastenation version of restrictivism, if no precise degree of fastenation among the xs marks the cut-off point for successful composition, then there are cases such that it is indeterminate whether an object exists that is composed of the xs. Restrictivism thus leads to indeterminacy of existence. This is indeterminacy of a very special sort. It is not merely indeterminate whether a given object is a knife. It is, rather, indeterminate whether there is an object in the first place. As is widely held, the term 'existence' is not semantically indeterminate. It has a precise meaning. Accordingly, indeterminacy of existence cannot be mere representational indeterminacy. It cannot be indeterminacy whose source lies in our access to the world. It must be indeterminacy in the world itself – it is *ontic*, or *metaphysical, indeterminacy*. And this type is widely eschewed as impossible. What holds for fastenation restrictivism holds for all versions of restrictivism that are sensitive to the manifest image, supporters of the indeterminacy objection claim: any attempt of specifying conditions of composition that are sensitive to the manifest image will have to countenance a grey area and hence ontic indeterminacy. This result, they maintain, goes too far. Restrictivism is to be abandoned.[7]

In response to this argument, one might go on a hunt for a natural, non-arbitrary compositional cut-off within the grey area. Intuitively, in our sorites series of fastenation, there is no specific degree, n, of fastenation between the handle and the blade such that the handle and the blade compose an object if and only if they are fastened together to degree n or higher. While this assessment is intuitively correct, untutored intuition may not be the best tool for detecting a compositional cut-off point. What the blunt notion of fastenation is meant to get at is causal interaction (of a sort that needs to be specified) among a plurality of things, the xs. Prima facie, a sorites series of states of causal interaction among the xs will not mark any of these states as special. When the series is described scientifically, however, one state in the series may well stand out with a special status, whatever that status may be. Perhaps it is the first state in the series in which the xs have a certain total energy (McKenzie & Muller, 2018). Those disturbed by ontic indeterminacy might thus hold that the impression of indeterminacy in a sorites series of composition is a mere illusion of common sense. When composition is approached scientifically, they might proclaim, there is a good chance that this indeterminacy disappears.

---

[7] For various approaches to ontic indeterminacy, see Akiba & Abasnezhad, 2014 and Hawley, 2002.

Is such a scientific contribution to battling ontic indeterminacy compatible with the manifest image? Suppose that we found a scientifically informed compositional cut-off in the sorites series involving the knife. And suppose that case II in Figure 3 falls on the non-compositional side of the cut-off: the degree of interaction between the handle and the blade in case II is too low for composition to occur. Suppose, moreover, that this cut-off is compatible with common sense since case II falls in the intuitive grey area of composition in this scenario. So, short of abandoning common sense completely, the scientific approach to SCQ steps in when common sense drops out. But now consider another example of an ordinary composite: a sofa, composed, inter alia, of a frame, a seat cushion, and a back cushion. This is a case where composition occurs determinately, we should think. The causal interaction between the frame and the cushion is, we may suppose, not stronger than the causal interaction between the handle and the blade in case II of our previous sorites series. However, in the sofa scenario, this degree of interaction occurs in an intuitively determinate case of composition, whereas in the knife scenario, the same degree occurs in an intuitively indeterminate case of composition. As a consequence, a precise compositional cut-off that captures the first case will not capture the second. Knives are in, sofas are out. The problem, in a nutshell, is that the intuitive compositional grey area is not always in the same place. This is a further indeterminacy problem for restrictivism, which a rigid scientific approach is ill-suited to handle.[8]

It is time to turn to mereological universalism, according to which, necessarily, for any plurality of objects, the xs, there exists an object composed of the xs. The mere existence of the xs is not only necessary (which is obvious) but also sufficient for composition. No further condition does any work in composition. Composition is a trivial matter. This answer to SCQ comes with the significant advantage that both objections to restrictivism considered earlier are avoided with ease. The specification objection causes no trouble for the obvious reason that there is or are no complicated condition or conditions to be specified. Existence, the only universalist condition on composition, is simple and absolute – or so universalists typically assume.[9]

The indeterminacy objection is not difficult to handle either. The bottom line on ontic indeterminacy is that universalism does not entail it because the universalist's condition on composition is clear-cut: when any xs exist, they compose something; there is no state of the xs such that it is indeterminate whether composition occurs. This is not the whole story on indeterminacy,

---

[8] For an overview of approaches to the indeterminacy objection, see Korman, 2010.
[9] More on different concepts of existence in Section 4.2.

though. Recall our initial sorites series for composition (Figure 3). Intuitively, it is indeterminate in case II whether the handle and the blade compose a knife. To honour the manifest image is to capture this indeterminacy. How can universalism account for it if there is no ontic indeterminacy? A popular answer is to treat this indeterminacy as representational. More specifically, the indeterminacy has its source in facts about the meaning of the noun 'knife'. In cases I, II, and III, there is determinately an object composed of the handle and the blade. Given the way in which 'knife' is used in ordinary language, the object in case III is a knife and the object in case I is not. However, ordinary usage of 'knife' does not fix whether the noun applies to the composite object in case II. This 'semantic indecision' (Lewis, 1986, p. 212) is the whole source of the intuitive indeterminacy in case II.

Furthermore, a straightforward account of the knife–sofa problem is available along the same lines. The problem, to repeat, is that the intuitive compositional grey area lies in different regions of the fastenation scale in the two scenarios. This difference does not come as a surprise if the source of the indeterminacy in the two scenarios is the semantic indeterminacy of ordinary sortal nouns. Ordinary usage of 'sofa' treats a composite whose parts are fastened together to degree n, for some n, as a clear case of application, whereas ordinary usage of 'knife' treats a composite whose parts are fastened together to degree n as an unclear case of application. The diagnosis of the grey area's shiftiness is just that the different sortal nouns have different grey areas of application.

Universalism faces its own objections. I shall look at two of them.

1.2.3 The Strangeness Objection

A worry about universalism that comes to mind immediately is that it entertains many strange objects that we would ordinarily reject. In our initial case, there is a knife, as expected, but there is also a knife-potato, a handle-potato, and a blade-potato. Common sense does not recognize these composites. Stranger still, there is a whole composed of the handle and Saturn and even a cross-categorial whole composed of Saturn and the letter-type 'L'.

Many universalists respond to the strangeness objection along the following lines. (I shall skirt subtle variations among different versions of the response.) Consider perceptual experience. When we perceive a certain scenario, we thereby have defeasible reason to hold that this scenario obtains. But when we do not perceive a certain scenario, we thereby have no reason to hold that the scenario fails to obtain. Perceptual experience has its limits. Analogously, the manifest image is a trustworthy guide to which material objects exist.

When the manifest image recognizes an object, we thereby have defeasible reason to hold that the object exists. But when the manifest image does not recognize an object, we thereby have no reason to hold that the object fails to exist. The manifest image has its limits. All the material objects recognized by common sense are contained in the universalist's domain of composites. All additional composites in that domain lie beyond the reach of common sense. The intuition that there is no object composed of the knife and the potato is to be understood as indicating that our ordinary concept of an object does not apply to a whole of the knife and the potato. The content of this concept marks the manifest image's limits. This is an outline of a response. The question ensues as to whether we really have such a concept, and if so, what the content of this concept is.[10]

1.2.4 The Economy Objection

The universalist's abundance of composites is suspect not only for reasons of common sense but also for reasons of theoretical economy. A methodological principle of considerable pedigree in metaphysics and elsewhere is that, in evaluating theories, simpler is better. When it comes to theoretical economy, universalism's plethora of composites puts the theory deep in the red. The versions of restrictivism considered earlier on, by contrast, yield a comparatively small domain of material objects and hence offer ontologically simpler theories. Of course, composition yields things over and above their parts. An addition of being by composition is not troubling in itself. What does cause concern is that universalism yields too many new objects. The realm of being ends up horribly overcrowded. Or so the objector complains.

One response to the economy objection is to argue that the composites recognized by universalism are, surprisingly, no addition of being. This result is achieved if composition is treated as a form of strict identity.[11] Upon this treatment, a composite is nothing over and above its parts – the composite just is them. Accordingly, composites are not to be counted in addition to their parts, and the economy objection loses its force. Strong composition as identity has received a fair amount of attention in recent years. It remains an exotic construction since, as various non-standard treatments of identity have shown in the past, getting creative with strict identity raises more questions than it answers.[12]

---

[10] For support of this response, see Sattig, 2015, ch. 2. For critical discussion, see Korman, 2008.

[11] This thesis is known as 'strong composition as identity'. For discussion, see Cotnoir & Baxte, 2014 and Wallace, 2011a, 2011b.

[12] See Hawthorne, 2006, ch. 1, for further discussion of non-standard views about identity.

Another response opens by questioning a key assumption in the economy objection, namely, the assumption that metaphysicians should strive for parsimony concerning what exists. While it is agreed that theoretical economy is to be upheld as a virtue in metaphysical theorizing, it is claimed that the focus of economical considerations should not be on what exists but rather on what is *fundamental*. Metaphysicians are in the business of explaining phenomena. When a fact (or proposition or statement) has a metaphysical explanation – a *ground* – then it is a *derivative* fact. When it has no such explanation, it is a fundamental fact. What metaphysicians should strive for is parsimony concerning unexplained, or fundamental, facts. They need not worry much, or not at all, about mere existence (Schaffer, 2009).[13]

How do these methodological considerations apply to universalism? Universalists are committed to an abundance of composite objects. By the aforementioned recommendation, their staggering number is no cause for concern. What we need to keep an eye on is whether the existence of these composites is derivative or fundamental. If their existence is fundamental, then universalism really is objectionably unparsimonious. Fortunately for universalists, it is quite natural to construe the many composites as derivative beings. For their existence can be given the following straightforward non-causal explanation: for any *x*s, the existence of the *x*s explains, or grounds, the existence of an object that is composed of the *x*s. By this move, universalism presents itself as highly explanatorily parsimonious. Notice, however, that the explanation of the existence of the whole by the existence of the parts is not entailed by universalism as stated initially. Standard universalism per se is not a principle about explanation – the 'if and only if' in the standard formulation is a mere material biconditional. The present proposal is a certain metaphysical interpretation of the universalist principle of composition. It is, to put a label on it, an account of composition as *generation*. By composing a whole the parts generate the whole. All it takes for the parts to generate the whole, according to universalism, is for them to exist. If restrictivism is interpreted generatively, by contrast, what it takes the parts to generate the whole is for them to satisfy a richer condition than mere existence. To emphasize, considerations of mereological generation play a role as soon as issues of metaphysical explanation, or grounding, come under discussion. Many other issues in the metaphysics of parthood do not require a stand on generation.[14]

---

[13] Another response that downplays the significance of mere existence is that an abundance in the number of things is less worrying than an abundance in the number of kinds or categories of things.

[14] Mereological generation has received relatively little discussion in contemporary metaphysics. See Fine, 2010 and Bennett, 2017, for exceptions.

1.3 Structured and Unstructured Objects

Consider a plurality of objects, the *x*s, and assume that the *x*s stand in the relation that in fact governs composition. So a material object, *o*, exists, which is composed of the *x*s. What is the *nature* of *o*? Alternatively put, what are *o*'s *essential properties*? These are familiar questions in metaphysics. They presuppose the view that things have essential properties, which is known as *essentialism*. Socrates, for instance, is a composite material object. What is his nature? That is, what properties are essential to him? Some essentialists hold that being a human organism is essential to him. How, then, are Socrates' parts related to his nature? In general, how are a material object's parts related to its nature? This question is the focus of this section. We thus move on from metaphysical issues concerning the relationship between the parts and the existence of objects to issues concerning the relationship between the parts and the nature of objects.

Two views will be distinguished: the view of objects as *unstructured* and the view of objects as *structured*. Suppose that an ordinary object, *o*, has objects *a* and *b* as proper parts. On one answer to our question, it is essential to *o* that *a* and *b* be parts of *o*. Object *o* belongs to some kind, as do *a* and *b*. Let *o* be the knife from previous sections, while *a* and *b* are the familiar handle and blade. On the view of objects as unstructured, the kind of *o* and the kinds of *a* and *b* make no contribution to *o*'s nature. Nor do any relations between *a* and *b* – such as the relation of fastenation – make any contribution to *o*'s nature. The nature of *o* depends on *which* objects *o* has as its parts, but not on how the parts are arranged or on what kinds they belong to. This makes *o* an unstructured object. What holds for *o* holds for all composite material objects.

By contrast, on a typical view of objects as structured, it is not essential to *o* that *a* and *b* be parts of *o*. Likewise for all other parts of *o*. Which objects are parts of *o* makes no contribution to *o*'s nature. What does, then? First, it is essential to *o* that it be a knife. Furthermore, it is essential to *o* that its parts belong to certain kinds and that they be arranged in a certain way. What kinds they must belong to and which arrangement they must exhibit depends on what kind of object *o* is. Thus, for *a* and *b* to be parts of *o*, they must belong to kinds that contribute to making *o* a knife – such as the kinds being a handle and being a blade – and they must be arranged in a way that likewise contributes to making *o* a knife – such as an arrangement of mutual fastenation. This makes *o* a structured object.[15]

---

[15] A friend of structured objects might hold that it is not only essential to *o* that its parts be arranged in a certain way, but also that it is essential to *o* that *a* and *b* be parts of *o*. Most structure lovers, however, hold that in typical cases it is not essential to *o* that particular objects be its parts. According to them, what matters for *o*'s nature is only its structure. Note also that some friends of structured objects (such as Fine, 2010) are not opposed to the existence of unstructured composites in addition to structured ones.

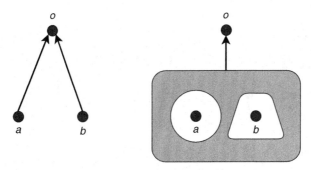

Figure 4 Unstructured versus structured objects

Some friends of structured objects characterize their view in figurative terms. A composite material object, *o*, is structured by a certain arrangement of *slots* that are *filled by* smaller material objects (Bennett, 2013; Sattig, 2019). The fillers of these slots are *o*'s proper parts. The idea that whether an *x* is a proper part of *o* depends on what kind of object *x* is can then be characterized in terms of slots: all slots of a material object are *kind-sensitive*. Moreover, the idea that whether some objects, the *x*s, compose *o* depends on how the *x*s are arranged can be characterized in terms of slots: *o*'s slots combine to constitute *o*'s *slot-structure*. The latter has also been described as *o*'s *form*, and the plurality of objects that fill *o*'s slots as *o*'s *matter*.[16] The view of composite objects as structured can thus be labelled a *hylomorphic* account of objects (Fine, 1999; Koslicki, 2008, 2018; Sattig, 2015). A simple schema of a slot-structure is illustrated in the right half of Figure 4, where the grey region stands for *o*'s slot-structure and the white regions inside of the grey one for slots of *o*. The figure contains an illustration of an unstructured object on the left-hand side. All dots below '*o*' stand for proper parts of *o*. Upward arrows indicate a contribution to *o*'s nature.[17]

The view of objects as structured is typically accompanied by the claim that an object's parts are *ordered hierarchically* – the claim, in other words, that an object has *immediate parts* and *mediate parts*. The handle and the blade are the knife's immediate parts, whereas the molecules in the handle and those in the blade are among the knife's mediate parts. This mereological hierarchy can be characterized in slot terms as well: *o* has *immediate slots* and *mediate slots*. The filler of the knife's handle slot and the filler of the knife's blade slot both have their own slots. The fillers of these may have further slots, and so on. An object's

---

[16] The notion of matter is not uniformly understood in this way.
[17] This essentialist interpretation of the arrow is to be distinguished from the more familiar interpretation of the arrow as standing for proper parthood.

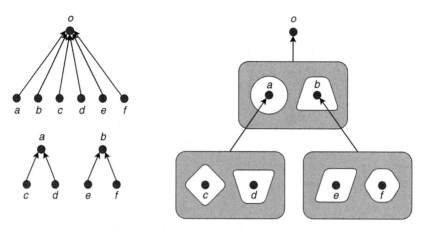

Figure 5 Flat versus hierarchical objects

immediate slot is a slot that the object has *simpliciter*, whereas an object's mediate slot is a slot of one of its slot fillers. By contrast, the view of objects as unstructured is typically combined with the claim that an object's parts are not ordered hierarchically. Instead, a composite object is mereologically *flat*. Here, each part of *o* makes exactly the same contribution to *o*'s nature. This difference is illustrated in Figure 5.[18]

Before discussing these positions further, let us take a step back and integrate them with the discussion of SCQ from Sections 1.1 and 1.2. Without going into any detail about their precise relationship – this is itself a controversial issue – mereological universalism about composition is a natural partner of the view of objects as unstructured. According to universalism, for any *x*s, all it takes for an object, *y*, composed of the *x*s to exist is for the *x*s to exist. This principle of composition combines naturally with the view that the essence of *y* depends only on *y*'s having the *x*s as parts. Neither the route from the parts to the whole nor the route from the whole to the parts involves any non-trivial properties or relations. Further, mereological restrictivism about composition is a natural partner of the view of objects as structured. According to restrictivism, a plurality of *x*s must have certain non-trivial properties or stand in certain non-trivial relations, in order for there to exist an object, *y*, that is composed of the *x*s. This combines naturally with the view that the essence of *y* depends on what its parts, the *x*s, are like and how they are arranged. Both the route from the parts

---

[18] The left-hand side of Figure 5 simplifies *o*'s mereological profile, for ease of illustration. The atomic parts of *o* are *c*, *d*, *e*, and *f*. If *o* lacks structure, then each sum of two or three elements from this list is also a proper part of *o*, and hence contributes to *o*'s nature. Among these parts only *c* + *d* (i.e. *a*) and *e* + *f* (i.e. *b*) are listed here.

to the whole and the route from the whole to the parts involve certain non-trivial properties or relations.

Let us now turn to the evaluation of the two positions on the structure of objects. Analogously to the three strategies of approaching SCQ, the issue of mereological structure can be approached in three different ways, namely, in light of the manifest image of objects, in the context of a general theory of parthood relations, and by recourse to scientific theories. The serious metaphysician will tackle the issue along all three dimensions. Let us set the second and third dimension aside here and just approach the issue along the first dimension.

By the lights of common sense are composite material objects structured or unstructured? Here are two considerations in support of their being structured. First, it might appear that the view of objects as unstructured clashes with the following pronouncement of common sense ordinary objects can and usually do change in their parts over time. For instance, a tree loses its leaves over time. When the tree is conceived of as an unstructured object, then it has all of its parts essentially. And so it seems that the tree cannot change in this way. By contrast, when the tree has just slots essentially, while it is inessential which objects fill these slots, then mereological change is possible. For different objects can fill the tree's slots at different moments. This worry concerns the persistence and change of material objects over time, which will be the topic of Section 2. As it will turn out in Section 2.2, the view of objects as unstructured is compatible with change in parts over time.

On to a more divisive consideration. Recall the knife from previous sections and suppose that a dried piece of potato is stuck to its blade. While the knife has the blade as a part, it does not have the piece of potato as a part. This seems obvious. How do we arrive at this pre-theoretical mereological judgement? We are quite good at parsing specific objects into their parts. Surely, in doing so we follow certain criteria. What are they?[19] Intuitively, the blade is a part of the knife because its being a blade contributes to making it a knife. The piece of potato, by contrast, is not a part of the knife because its being a piece of potato does not contribute at all to making it a knife. Similarly, the wheel on the back seat of a car is not a part of the car because this wheel is not connected to other parts of the car in a way that contributes to making it a car – because, that is, the wheel does not play the role of a wheel in this car.

These pre-theoretical criteria by which we seem to parse an ordinary object into parts favour the view of objects as structured. Only on the latter view, parthood is a kind-sensitive and arrangement-sensitive concept: whether some

---

[19] This question is not to be answered from the armchair alone. Psychologists should have a say as well. What I offer here is to be regarded as a hypothesis.

x is a part of a given object depends on what kind *x* belongs to, and on how *x* is related to certain other objects. On the view of objects as unstructured, it is simply false that the blade is a part of the knife because its being a blade contributes to the whole's being a knife. Notice that opponents of structure can still accept that something's being a blade contributes to something's being a knife – that is, they can accept that there is an explanatory link between these kinds. But they cannot accept that parthood is governed by this sort of link. To repeat, the common-sense concept of parthood seems to be kind-sensitive and arrangement-sensitive. Only the view of objects as structured honours this aspect of the manifest image.

Furthermore, it is very natural for ordinary thinkers to conceive of certain wholes as hierarchical. Intuitively, the branch is a part of the tree. And since the leaf is a part of the branch, the leaf is a part of the tree. Similarly, the wires are parts of the piano because they are parts of a string and this string is a part of the piano. Given that ordinary criteria of parthood are kind-sensitive, these intuitions reflect that we judge the parts of a given whole as being more or less relevant to what kind of object the whole is. The branch is more immediately relevant to the tree than the leaf. Since, according to the view of objects as unstructured, all wholes are flat, this view is in tension with our ordinary conception of certain wholes as hierarchical. Summing up, if the way in which we ordinarily parse objects is taken at face value, then the metaphysical account of material objects as structured is in a better position to capture the manifest image of objects than the view of objects as unstructured. As ever, it is controversial whether and to what extent the manifest image is to be considered relevant to metaphysics.

While the view of objects as structured honours common sense, many metaphysicians find it hard to accept. One reason for resistance is simply that the view is difficult to understand. One cannot be blamed for struggling with the idea that ordinary objects have a form that carves out slots filled by the object's parts. Everyone agrees that this is no more than a picture. What exactly does it mean?[20] Another reason for resistance is that the view of objects as unstructured has a much simpler architecture than the hylomorphic picture with its byzantine excess of slots and mereological levels.

Lack of intelligibility and simplicity are not the only reasonable concerns about structured objects. Here is a further reason for being sceptical about the view. Many metaphysicians are attracted to the thought that all ordinary macrophysical objects derive their existence from microphysical facts, such as facts about the arrangements of physical particles. Is this popular thought compatible

---

[20] See Sattig, 2019, for a reductive account of an object's slot-structure.

with the view of objects as structured? It seems not. Consider, for instance, a tree, and suppose that it is a structured object. If the tree derives its very being from certain microphysical facts, then essentialists should expect that these facts contribute to the nature of the tree. Given that the tree is structured – where mereological structure is understood along the lines sketched earlier – the tree does not derive its being from any facts about particular particles. For the tree's nature is not sensitive to any particular particles. If the tree does in fact have certain particles as parts, then it could fail to have these particles as parts – that is, its micro-level mereological slots could be filled by different particles. Similarly, the tree does not derive its being from any facts about the properties or arrangement of particles at any particular time or in any particular place. For the tree's essential slot-structure is not sensitive to any particular time nor to any particular place. If the tree does in fact have certain micro-parts at a certain time, in a certain place, then it could fail to have the parts at this time, in this place. It follows from these considerations that the tree would have to derive its being from non-particular microphysical facts, such as the fact that some particles instantiate a tree-wise arrangement in some place, at some time. It is implausible, however, that any particular tree derives its being entirely from non-particular facts. Hence, it seems that a structured tree does not derive its being from microphysical facts at all. An unstructured tree, by contrast, derives its being from microphysical facts in a straightforward fashion: the mere existence of a certain plurality of physical particles grounds the existence of our tree. Correspondingly, each of the particles is an essential part of the tree. The picture of ordinary macrophysical objects as derivative beings thus requires these objects to be unstructured.[21]

2 Persistence

The temporal profile of material objects raises a number of issues that have received much attention in recent metaphysics. We will begin, in Section 2.1, with the formulation of two questions about the persistence of objects and that of a range of answers to these questions. Subsequently, in Sections 2.2 and 2.3, these answers will be discussed in connection with various considerations about change.

2.1 Endurance and Perdurance

Material objects, such as persons, trees, and tables, *persist* through time. That is, they exist at different moments of time. In what follows, I shall consider two

---

[21] For further discussion of hylomorphism about material objects, see Evnine, 2016; Fine, 1999, 2010; Koslicki, 2008, 2018; Sattig, 2015, 2019.

metaphysical questions about the persistence of material objects and various answers.

2.1.1 First Question: How Does a Continuant Persist Through Time?

A persisting material object will be called a *continuant*. David Lewis (1986, p. 202) famously asked the question how a continuant persists through time. This question generalizes across different kinds of continuant. It is thus to be distinguished from the following kind-oriented question: How do continuants of a given kind, such as persons, persist through time? In other words, under what conditions does a continuant of a given kind come into existence and under what conditions does it go out of existence? This sort of question concerns what are often called the conditions, or criteria, of persistence for certain kinds of continuant. Philosophers also speak of criteria of identity over time, such as the criteria of personal identity. I shall set kind-oriented questions of persistence aside for now. These will be discussed in later sections.

Lewis (1986, p. 202) formulated two answers to his question. The first answer is that a continuant persists through an interval of time by having a *temporal part* at each moment in the interval. In this case, Lewis says, the object *perdures*. The perdurance of an object is often compared to the way in which an event, such as a concert, is spread out through time. If a subject attends a concert at a moment, *t*, all that the subject really experiences at *t* is a momentary stage of the concert. Analogously, if a subject looks at a perduring tree at *t*, all that the subject really sees at *t* is a momentary stage, a temporal part, of the tree. (Since the subject perdures as well, what strictly has the experience at *t* is a temporal part of the subject.) The second answer is that a continuant persists through an interval by being *wholly present* at each moment in the interval. In this case, Lewis says, the object *endures*. If a subject looks at an enduring tree at *t*, the subject really sees the tree, not just a momentary stage of it. (And it is the enduring subject itself, not just a temporal part of it, that strictly has the experience at *t*.) The view that continuants perdure is known as *perdurantism*, and the view that they endure as *endurantism*.[22]

These accounts of persistence are in need of further elaboration. Let us begin with perdurantism. What is a temporal part of an object? Intuitively, just as a spatially extended object is divided into different spatial parts, so a persisting object is divided into different temporal parts. The standard definition of a temporal part of an object at a moment employs the notions of having a part

---

[22] The labels 'four-dimensionalism' and 'three-dimensionalism' are sometimes used in place of 'perdurantism' and 'endurantism', respectively (Sider, 2001). I shall not use them here.

at a moment and of existing at a moment. Since temporal parts feature in the perdurantist explanation of what existing at a moment consists in, the notion of temporal parthood must not itself be defined in terms of the same notion of existing at a moment, on pain of circularity. So let us distinguish an ordinary notion of existing at a moment – in terms of which persistence is defined – from a technical notion of *existing at* a moment (marked by italics). While the latter is intended to be the basic notion linking existence and moments, which all parties in the debate are meant to accept, the ordinary notion is a non-basic notion that is explained in different ways by different parties. Then we can give the following definition: for any x, y, and t,

x is an *instantaneous temporal part* of y at $t = {}_{df}$ (1) x *exists at*, but only *at*, t; (2) x is a part of y at t; and (3) x overlaps at t everything that is a part of y at t.[23]

Intuitively, a table's temporal part at a moment, t, is a part of the table at t, which is confined to t, and which is as big as the table is at t. It is a short-lived table-shaped slice, or *stage*, of a table.

Perdurantism is the view that a continuant exists at a moment – in the ordinary sense – only in a *derivative* way. It does not *exist at* a moment in the most basic sense. It rather exists at a moment, in virtue of having a temporal part at that moment, which *exists at* that moment in the most basic sense. (I shall elaborate on the more basic notion later in this section.)

In Sections 1.1 and 1.2, we encountered SCQ and the distinction between unrestricted and restricted composition. Back then we ignored the temporal dimension of objects. If the persistence of objects is taken into account, and if objects perdure, SCQ splits into two questions – one about synchronic composition and one about diachronic composition. First, under what conditions do some simultaneous stages compose a further stage? Second, under what conditions do some non-simultaneous stages compose a continuant? A common addition to perdurantism is the view of synchronic and diachronic composition as unrestricted: for any plurality of simultaneous or non-simultaneous stages, there is an object that is composed of these stages. As a result of this view, there is an abundance of perduring continuants, which far exceeds the number of continuants recognized by common sense.

In Section 1.3, we encountered the distinction between structured and unstructured objects, which concerns the issue of how an object's parts relate to the object's nature or essence. The scope of this issue can be extended to include the temporal profile of material objects. How do the parts of a continuant at different moments relate to the absolute, timeless nature of the continuant? The default view among perdurantists is that continuants are

---

[23] Adapted from Sider, 2001, p. 59.

unstructured wholes of temporal and spatial parts. While unstructured wholes have all of their parts essentially, it is still possible for unstructured wholes with temporal parts to undergo mereological change in the ordinary sense of change, as will become apparent in Section 2.2. As I pointed out in Section 1.3, unrestricted composition and unstructuredness are natural partners. Note, though, that the other natural combination, of restricted composition and structuredness, is also an option for perdurantists. If perduring continuants are unstructured, a further reasonable addition to perdurantism is the view that composition is generative: the parts generate the whole. As a consequence of this view, a continuant's temporal parts are more fundamental than, or explanatorily prior to, the whole.[24]

Moving on to the clarification of endurantism, the main task is to specify what it means for an object to be wholly present at a moment, such that a continuant's existing at t consists in its being wholly present at t. This turns out to be a difficult task.[25] Under what conditions is 'all of' an object, x, present at a moment, t? Everyone (including the perdurantist) agrees that all the parts that x has at t are around at t. If this is what being wholly present means, then being wholly present is a trivial matter of no interest to metaphysics. Alternatively, one might propose that x is wholly present at t just in case any object that is a part of x at any moment is also a part of x at t. Combining endurantism with this definition has the consequence that, necessarily, a continuant has the same parts at all moments at which it exists. This consequence is to be avoided, however, since many continuants change their parts over time. As a reaction to the difficulty involved in defining the notion of being wholly present, a number of metaphysicians have recommended a simplification of Lewis' formulation of endurantism along the following lines: a continuant exists at different moments, but it does not exist at these moments by having different temporal parts at the different moments.

How do endurantists typically approach the mereological issues of Section 1 when these are discussed in application to continuants? Very briefly, the default view among endurantists on the conditions of composition is that composition is restricted: necessarily, for any xs, and any moment t, there is an object composed of the xs at t iff the xs stand in a certain non-trivial relation at t. Further, the default view of endurantists on the question of mereological structure is that continuants are structured wholes. As I pointed out in Section 1.3, restricted composition and structuredness are natural partners. The other natural

---

[24] The claim that a continuant's atemporal existence derives from the atemporal existence of its parts goes beyond the key claim of perdurantism that a continuant exists at a moment, in virtue of having a temporal part at that moment.

[25] See Sider, 2001, pp. 63–8. See Wasserman, 2016, for further discussion.

combination, of unrestricted composition and unstructuredness, is also a consistent option for endurantists. The latter option, however, threatens to rule out the possibility for an enduring continuant to undergo mereological change. As an unstructured object, an enduring continuant, x, has all of its parts essentially. Hence, necessarily, any object that is a part of x at any moment is a part of x throughout x's life. (More on change in Section 2.2.)

2.1.2 Second Question: How Is a Continuant Located in Spacetime?

So far, we have taken the temporal moments of ordinary thought and talk at face value. Let us now look at these moments under the metaphysical microscope. Spacetime theories in modern physics do not begin with times and places. They begin with *spacetime points*, which are understood as instantaneous, spatially unextended, and partless things. In so-called *classical* spacetimes, relations of temporal distance among (spacetime) points are well defined. Any points p and q have a certain temporal distance. If the distance is zero, then p and q are simultaneous; otherwise, p is earlier than q or p is later than q. Each plurality of points has a sum. This is a *spacetime region*. The sum of a plurality that contains all simultaneous points is a *hyperplane of simultaneity*. A classical spacetime permits a division, or foliation, into a unique plurality of three-dimensional, non-overlapping hyperplanes of simultaneity. These hyperplanes are our familiar moments of time, as conceived of by classical physics. This account of temporal moments is illustrated in Figure 6, where each rectangular solid corresponds to a hyperplane.

In ordinary circumstances, we say that a material object, such as Socrates, exists at a plurality of moments, and that he is located at a certain spatial region at each of these moments. The plurality of pairs of a place and a moment at which Socrates finds himself throughout his life corresponds to a geometrically four-dimensional region of spacetime. Let us call it Socrates' *path*. This region has a unique division into non-overlapping instantaneous regions, each of which is a part of a particular hyperplane, or moment. Let us call them *path-slices*. These preliminaries allow the formulation of our second metaphysical question: How is a persisting material object located at its path through spacetime?

Two answers to this question have been discussed intensely. It is common to formulate these answers with the help of the following concept. An object is *exactly located* at a (spacetime) region just in case the object has the same shape and size as the region, and stands in the same spatiotemporal relations as the region. The first answer to our question is that each continuant is exactly located at its four-dimensional path. Since the path is temporally

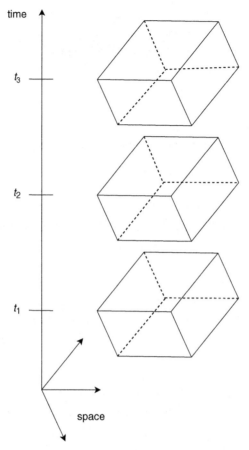

Figure 6 Moments as hyperplanes of simultaneity

extended, in virtue of having path-slices that belong to different hyperplanes, so is the continuant. The second answer to our question is that no persisting material object is exactly located at its path, and hence no object is temporally extended. Instead, a continuant is exactly located at each instantaneous slice of its path. To emphasize, while the path-slices compose a four-dimensional region, the object is exactly located at the slices without being exactly located at the whole region. On the first answer, a material object is *singly located* in spacetime, whereas on the second answer, a material object is *multi-located* in spacetime.[26]

---

[26] Discussions of these views on persistence and spatiotemporal location go back to Gilmore, 2006, and Sattig, 2006. The concept of exact location receives a critical discussion in Parsons, 2007. Multi-location is discussed, inter alia, in Balashov, 2010, Calosi & Costa, 2015, Donnelly, 2010, Eagle, 2016, and Gilmore, 2008.

Let us connect the second question with the first. According to perdurantism, a continuant, o, exists at a moment, t, by having a temporal part at t. Given that a moment is a hyperplane of simultaneity, o has a temporal part at t by having a temporal part that is exactly located at a subregion of t. The sum of all instantaneous regions at which o's temporal parts are exactly located is o's four-dimensional path. If we take the exact location of a whole to be the sum of the exact locations of its parts – as seems plausible in the absence of multi-location – it follows that o is exactly located at its path, and hence that o is temporally extended. Thus, there is a natural route from perdurantism – a mereological thesis – to the view of continuants as temporally extended – a locational thesis. Notice, though, that the locational thesis does not entail the mereological thesis. The combination of perdurantism with temporal extension is illustrated in Figure 7.

According to endurantism, no continuant exists at any moment by having a temporal part at that moment. Given that moments are hyperplanes of simultaneity, and given the notion of exact location, endurantist existence at

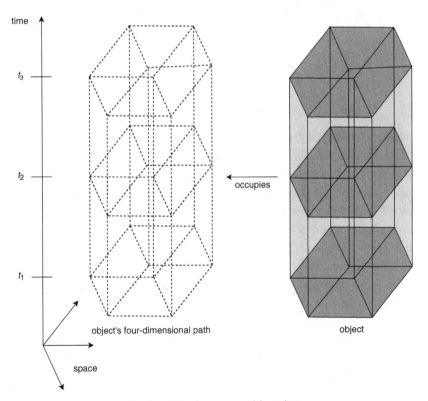

Figure 7 Perdurance and location

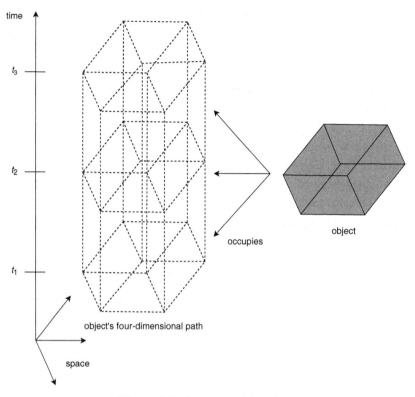

time

t_3

t_2

occupies

object

t_1

object's four-dimensional path

space

Figure 8 Endurance and location

a moment lends itself to a straightforward analysis: o exists at t just in case o is exactly located at a subregion of t.[27] Since o persists, it follows that o is *multi-located* in spacetime. Assuming that o is multi-located across its path without also being exactly located at its path, o is temporally unextended. While the mereological thesis of endurantism and the locational view of continuants as temporally unextended are independent of one another, the mentioned combination is a natural one. The combination of endurantism with multi-location is illustrated in Figure 8.

These two packages of claims are not without alternatives. One frequently discussed alternative should be mentioned here as well. The standard *stage view* shares its foundations with the perdurantist package (Hawley, 2001; Sider, 2001). Instantaneous stages are exactly located at instantaneous regions of spacetime. For any plurality of such stages, there is a whole composed of

---

[27] The notion of being exactly located at a subregion of t plays the same role, in a spacetime framework, as the more neutral primitive notion of *existence at t* introduced earlier.

them. Such a whole is temporally extended: it exactly occupies the four-dimensional region composed of the instantaneous regions exactly occupied by its temporal parts. These are the similarities.[28] In contrast to perdurantism, the stage view denies that an ordinary object, such as a tree or a table, is a temporally extended whole. Rather, an ordinary object is just an instantaneous stage, and hence it is temporally unextended. Does this mean that an ordinary object fails to persist? No. Where the standard perdurantist sees one temporally extended tree with many instantaneous temporal parts, the stage lover sees many trees, where each instantaneous tree is a *temporal counterpart* of all the others and of itself. Moreover, for a tree to exist at a moment, *t* – in the ordinary sense of existence at a moment – is for it to have a temporal counterpart at *t*. As a consequence, each instantaneous tree derivatively exists at all the moments, at which we would ordinarily expect it to exist – each tree persists through time. In a nutshell, while an ordinary object is exactly located at no more than a single instantaneous spacetime region, it persists through time, in virtue of having temporal counterparts at other moments. This is the core of the stage view.

While the stage view belongs to the same family as perdurantism, due to the central theoretical role it assigns to temporally unextended material objects, the former is more radical than the latter, by the lights of common sense. For each ordinary object, the perdurantist sees many temporal parts that are not recognized pre-philosophically. This fact, however, need not be treated as a significant shortcoming. Ordinary thinkers, the perdurantist may reply, are just not sophisticated enough to recognize all the temporal parts that an object has. The theme is familiar from Section 1: the manifest image has its limits. The stage view, by contrast, does not merely transgress the manifest image of objects, but is forced to revise it. For example, I am currently sitting on a chair. How many chairs have I been sitting on over the course of the past hour? According to intuition, the answer is 'one'. According to the stage view, the answer is 'indefinitely many'. Despite this radical departure from common sense, stage lovers take their view to boast significant virtues. I shall discuss one of these in Section 3.2. Until then, the stage view will be set aside.[29]

As this review of metaphysical questions about persistence draws to a close, it remains to address a common presupposition of all positions that have been formulated here. The presupposition concerns the nature of time. The foregoing discussion of persistence assumed that all the moments at which objects exist are ontologically on a par; each moment exists in the most basic sense of

---

[28] Strictly speaking, the stage view is only committed to stages, not to their fusion. But most stage lovers accept such fusions.

[29] For two further non-standard accounts of persistence, see Costa, 2017, and Sattig, 2015.

'existence'. In the philosophy of time, this view is known as *eternalism*. Eternalism is encoded in the account of moments as hyperplanes of simultaneity in a four-dimensional spacetime, in which each point and region is equally real. While eternalism ranks as orthodoxy, it is not the only game in town. The most widely discussed non-eternalist picture of time is *presentism*, according to which the present moment is metaphysically privileged vis-à-vis past and future moments. Many presentists hold that, in the most basic sense of 'existence', only the present moment exists. Our two metaphysical questions about persistence were discussed on the assumption of eternalism. If these questions are debated on the assumption of presentism instead, or of other non-eternalist pictures of time, some answers we encountered might not be available anymore, while new answers might present themselves. The interaction of the metaphysics of persistence with the metaphysics of time is an important topic, but one that cannot be discussed appropriately in the confines of this Element.

In the remainder of Section 2, the perdurantist package and the endurantist package characterized earlier will be tested in application to various metaphysical issues regarding change.

2.2 Change and Collapse

As an object persists, it *changes*: it has different, incompatible properties (or relations) at different moments at which it exists. For instance, an arm has a straight shape at one moment and a bent shape at another. Just as we previously asked how continuants persist, we can now ask how continuants change. This is widely known as the *problem of change*.[30] One's answer to this question will depend on one's account of persistence, and will therefore be relevant to debates about persistence.

Let us begin with the explanation of change offered by perdurantism. A material object, o, exists at a moment, t, by having a temporal part at t. Assuming this account of persistence, o has a property, φ, for any φ, at t by having an instantaneous temporal part at t, which has φ simpliciter. Since an instantaneous temporal part does not persist, it need not be described as having a property at a moment. It is more accurately described as having the property atemporally, or as having it *simpliciter*. Since a perduring continuant has a property at a moment only derivatively, it changes only derivatively. Its having different properties at different moments is grounded in its having different temporal parts at these moments, which have the properties simpliciter. The

---

[30] A more restricted version is known as the 'problem of temporary intrinsics'. For a discussion of the problem of change, see Eddon, 2010; Haslanger, 1989; Hinchliff, 1996; Hofweber, 2009; Lewis, 1986, 1988; Sattig, 2006, ch. 3; Sider, 2001, sect. 4.6.

temporal sensitivity of the instantiation of a property is thus superficial. It disappears upon analysis. An arm that changes in shape has a temporal part with an atemporal straight shape and another temporal part with an atemporal bent shape.

Notice that the same schema applies to mereological change: a tree, o, has a certain leaf, l, as a part at one moment, t_1, but lacks it as a part at another moment, t_2, because o's temporal part at t_1 has l's temporal part at t_1 as a part simpliciter, while o's temporal part at t_2 does not have l's temporal part at t_2 as a part simpliciter. Since mereological change is derivative, a perduring whole can change its parts, even if it is an unstructured object, and hence has all of its parts essentially. The issue of whether the combination of unstructuredness and mereological change is possible came up in Sections 1.3 and 2.1.

How can endurantists explain change? Prima facie, episodes of change involve temporally sensitive instantiations of properties – that is, the relevant properties are instantiated at a moment. While perdurantists reduce this temporal sensitivity to instantiation simpliciter, endurantists must treat it as irreducible. Here is why. Since, according to endurantism, a continuant, o, exists at a moment, t, in a way that does not rely on its having a temporal part at t, o's having a property at t cannot derive from an instantaneous temporal part's having the property simpliciter. The involvement of t in o's having a property at t cannot be explained in the following straightforward fashion, either: o has φ at t because o exists at t and because o has φ simpliciter. This is not an option, since an object with incompatible properties, φ and ψ, at different moments would end up being φ and ψ simpliciter, which is impossible.

What more can be said about o's having φ at t, given that o changes with respect to φ, and given that the temporal sensitivity of this fact is irreducible? The most widely discussed endurantist account is that o has φ at t, for any φ and t because o stands in the φ-*relation* to t. When my left arm changes in shape from t_1 to t_2, the arm stands in the straight-shape-relation to t_1, while standing in the bent-shape-relation to t_2. The qualities that appear as shape-properties on the surface turn out, upon metaphysical analysis, to be shape-relations to temporal moments.

Lewis (1986, pp. 202–4, 1988) famously complained that the account of shapes and other changeable physical attributes as relations to moments is implausible. Let us consider his widely discussed thoughts on shape. What is so objectionable about shape-relations to moments? Lewis' first pass is that, intuitively, shapes are *intrinsic* to material objects, while shape-relations to moments are not. Few have been gripped by this objection. Here is a common intuitive test for intrinsicality: a property or relation is intrinsic to an object just in case we can imagine the object as having the property or relation while being alone in the universe. Arguably, this test classifies shape-relations to moments as intrinsic, *pace* Lewis' complaint, since imagining an object as being alone in the universe still requires imagining it as being immersed in space and time. Thus, cosmic solitude does not prevent an object from having shape-relations to moments.

Lewis' second pass is that shapes should be understood as properties that are had *simpliciter*. Since, by the lights of common sense, to change in shape is to have incompatible shapes at different moments, the objection is sensible only if it concerns the explanation, or ground, of ordinary shape-change: shape-change should, according to Lewis, be explainable in terms of having a shape simpliciter – that is, in a temporally insensitive fashion. An endurantist who views shapes as relations that are irreducibly pointed towards some moment, by virtue of taking a moment as a relatum, cannot satisfy this desideratum. The latter is satisfied straightforwardly, by contrast, if having a shape at a moment is grounded in having a temporal part who has that shape simpliciter. Fair enough, an endurantist might reply. But why should we accept this explanatory desideratum in the first place? Lewis does not motivate it. He just puts it out there.

Support for the desideratum is available, if we inspect shapes under the metaphysical microscope. Suppose that my left arm has a certain shape at t. The arm is composed of a plurality of microphysical particles at t. These particles stand in certain relations of spatial distance to each other at t. Now, it is quite plausible to understand the shape of the arm at t as consisting in the pattern of spatial distance-relations among the arm's micro-parts at t.[31] This is a reductive explanation of shapes in terms of spatial distance-relations. Focus, next, on distance-relations among particles at t. Assuming that particles α and β are exactly located at spatial points p and q at t, respectively, α and β stand in a certain distance-relation at t by *inheriting* this relation from p and q: α and β are, say, five millimetres apart at t, because α exactly occupies p at t, β exactly occupies q at t, and p is five millimetres apart from q at t. Notice now that in a classical four-dimensional spacetime, p and q are five millimetres apart at t because p's temporal part at t and q's temporal part t are five millimetres apart simpliciter. (Many endurantists accept that spacetime regions have temporal parts.) Thus, α and β's standing in a spatial distance-relation at t is naturally explained in terms of the instantiation of this relation simpliciter. The endurantist who adopts the relational account of shape-change cannot accept this explanation. According to her, an object's having a shape is irreducibly pointed towards a moment. Her two-place shape-relations to a moment can at best be reduced to three-place distance-relations among particles and a moment. This is

---

[31] See Gibson & Pooley, 2006, p. 162; Pooley, 2019.

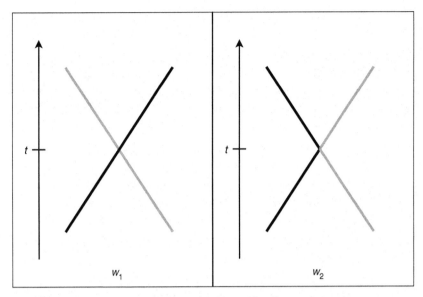

Figure 9 The problem of collapse

one way of supporting Lewis' complaint against the relational account of change. I shall leave this site by emphasizing that the relational account is not the only option available to endurantists. Accordingly, we should refrain from concluding, on the mentioned grounds alone, that the problem of change gives perdurantism a decisive advantage.

From a change-based attack on endurantism, we shall now turn to a change-based attack on perdurantism. In this case, we shall focus on the motion of continuants. Imagine the following two possibilities, illustrated in Figure 9. In one possible world, w_1, two particles move towards each other. At the moment, t, at which their paths intersect, they co-locate and subsequently move away from each other in the direction in which they approached each other before t. In another possible world, w_2, two particles move towards each other. At the moment, t, at which their paths intersect, they co-locate, 'bounce', and then move away from each other in the direction originally taken by the partner.[32] We can thus distinguish in thought a possibility involving only particles with straight paths from a possibility involving only particles with angular paths. Any metaphysical account of persistence and motion should be able to sustain this distinction.

On the popular 'at-at theory of motion', a continuant moves by having different spatial locations at different moments. According to perdurantism,

---

[32] This case is due to Hawthorne (2006, p. 121).

a continuant has a certain spatial location at a moment by having a temporal part at that moment, which has the location simpliciter. As was pointed out in Section 2.1, perdurantists typically adopt mereological universalism, according to which, for any plurality of instantaneous stages, there is a whole composed of these stages. The combination of these assumptions threatens to collapse the difference between w_1 and w_2. In w_1, there are two continuants with straight paths. Call the two particles in w_1 'α' and 'β', respectively. The temporal parts of α before t and the temporal parts of β after t compose a continuant with an angular path. Similarly, the temporal parts of β before t and the temporal parts of α after t compose a continuant with an angular path. On analogous grounds, w_2 contains two continuants with straight paths. It seems, therefore, that both worlds contain continuants with straight paths and continuants with angular paths, and hence that the difference between the two possibilities collapses. This is an instance of the *problem of collapse.*[33]

Perdurantists can avail themselves of the following response. The difference between w_1 and w_2 is not that w_1 contains only continuants with straight paths, while w_2 contains only continuants with angular paths. The difference is, rather, that w_1 contains only continuants of a certain kind with straight paths, while w_2 contains only continuants of this kind with angular paths. For simplicity, let the relevant kind be the kind *particle*: w_1 contains only particles with straight paths; w_2 contains only particles with angular paths. While there are more continuants in w_1 and w_2, they are not particles.

So far, so good. But what makes a perduring continuant belong to the relevant kind? The following answer will not do. Assume that there is a natural property, φ, which plays a certain role in physics, and that an object is a particle just in case it has φ at each moment of its life. Given the perdurantist account of having a property at a moment introduced earlier, the proposed ground of being a particle is insufficient to sustain the intended difference between w_1 and w_2. In w_1, there are perduring continuants with straight paths and those with angular paths. Since each of these continuants is composed of temporal parts that have φ, each is a particle, by the proposal under consideration. Likewise for w_2. Hence, both worlds contain particles with straight paths and ones with angular paths.

A popular alternative is to appeal to causation. There are different versions of the causal response to the collapse problem. On the simplest version, it is

---

[33] The label is Hawthorne's (2006, ch. 6). The most famous collapse scenario is the Kripke/ Armstrong rotating disc (Armstrong, 1980). The present case has the advantage of not relying on homogeneity. For discussion, see Butterfield, 2005; Hawthorne, 2006, ch. 6; Lewis, 1999; Sider, 2001, sect. 6.5; Zimmerman, 1998, 1999.

assumed that there is a special causal relation, known as *immanent causation*, which holds between certain instantaneous stages and not others (Zimmerman, 1997). The perdurantist may then say that a whole composed of stages is a particle just in case it is maximally interrelated by immanent causation – that is, just in case each stage in the whole is linked, immediately or mediately, by this cross-temporal relation to every other stage in the whole. The expectation driving this proposal is that all causally interrelated wholes in w_1 have straight paths, while all causally interrelated wholes in w_2 have angular paths. This is not the case, however, for the following reason. In w_1, α and β are co-located at t – that is, they exactly occupy the same place at t. Perdurantists will want to say that α and β are co-located at t by having a common temporal part at t.[34] This shared stage is causally linked to all temporal parts of α and β before and after t. Analogously for w_2. Therefore, w_1 and w_2 contain both maximally causally interrelated wholes with straight paths and those with angular paths. Again, the difference collapses.

Theodore Sider (2001, pp. 224–36) proposed a version of the causal response, according to which stages are not grouped into particles by local properties of them or local relations among them. Instead, stages are grouped into particles globally – that is, by recourse to what happens across an entire possible world. Adopting Lewis' *best-system theory* of laws of nature, Sider suggests that the correct grouping of stages into particles is the one 'that results in the best candidate set of laws of dynamics' (2001, p. 230). Thus, the perdurantist gets to say that w_1 contains only particles with straight paths, because this grouping of stages into particles fits best with the simplest and explanatorily most powerful dynamical generalizations in w_1. And analogously for particles with angular paths in w_2. Addressing the details of this account would lead us irresponsibly deep into the metaphysics of causation and laws of nature. Suffice it to say that while Sider's proposal is elegant and effective, it has its limits. As he admits, the strategy is powerless when w_1 and w_2 are extremely simple worlds containing nothing but the two particles.[35]

Endurantists are in a position to deal with the collapse problem in a different way. The most straightforward endurantist response is the following. In order to capture the intuitive difference between w_1 and w_2, endurantists must maintain that all particles in w_1 have straight paths, while all particles in w_2 have angular paths. Why does w_1 not also contain particles with angular paths? And why does w_2 not also contain particles with straight paths? The simple answer is that it is a basic, contingent fact about w_1 that all continuants in w_1 have straight paths,

---

[34] This view on co-location will be relevant to the issues discussed in Section 3.

[35] Friends of the Humean best-system theory of laws will not be shattered by this limitation. They are quite accustomed to the breakdown of their account when applied to simple worlds.

and also a basic, contingent fact about w_2 that all continuants in w_2 have angular paths. Endurantists can avail themselves of this answer because their explanations of the temporal profiles of material objects start at the level of continuants. They do not start at the level of instantaneous stages, from which continuants are 'built', as standard perdurantists do. Therefore, they do not face the situation that there is, by mereological universalism, an 'automatic' abundance of continuants that threaten to collapse the difference between our two worlds.

Yet endurantists can, and some do, recognize an abundance of continuants in w_1 and w_2. According to them, w_1 contains both continuants with straight paths and continuants with angular paths; and likewise for w_2. While these endurantists face the same collapse-threatening plurality of continuants as standard perdurantists, they are able to avoid collapse in a natural way, which is not available to perdurantists. Here is how. Assume that an object is a particle just in case it is *essentially* φ, for some natural property or cluster of natural properties φ. In w_1, there are two continuants, α and β, with straight paths, which are both φ throughout their lives. In w_1, there are, in addition, two continuants, γ and δ, with angular paths, which are also both φ throughout their lives, such that γ is co-located with α before t and with β after t, while δ is co-located with β before t and with δ after t. Yet only α and β are φ essentially, whereas γ and δ are φ merely accidentally (whatever their essential properties might be). Thus, only α and β are particles. In w_2, we have the same plurality of continuants, all of which are φ throughout their lives. But here only the continuants with angular paths are φ essentially, and hence only they are particles. Collapse avoided. The soul of this response is the acceptance of kind-related fundamental facts about the nature or essence, of continuants.[36] Since perdurantists typically deny that any continuants in w_1 and w_2 have any physical properties relevant to being a particle essentially, they cannot appeal to the essentialist concept of a particle invoked in this response. Importantly, the essentialist assumption doing the main work for abundance-loving endurantists is not ad hoc. It is not a device introduced specifically to deal with the collapse problem. As we saw in Section 1.3, the essential properties of material objects play a systematic role in the sort of metaphysical picture of objects favoured by many endurantists. To conclude, the present treatment of the collapse problem is smoother than any strategy available to perdurantists. And it applies to simple worlds as well.

---

[36] As a variant of this response, one might hold that while, in w_1, all continuants are particles, only α and β are particles essentially, whereas γ and δ are particles accidentally. This variant will be preferred by those who hold that an object is a particle just in case it is φ, for some natural property or cluster of natural properties φ.

2.3 Persistence and Relativity

The theory of relativity raises a number of philosophical challenges regarding persistence. One such challenge concerns what might be called *relativistic change*. First, a few basics. In a relativistic spacetime – such as *Minkowski spacetime* – simultaneity and temporal duration are not invariant notions. It is not meaningful to ask whether two spacetime points are simultaneous or whether one is separated from the other by some temporal interval. An *inertial reference frame* in a relativistic spacetime is given, roughly, by a collection of objects that do not accelerate and that are at rest with respect to each other. Relative to each inertial frame, the spacetime has a unique foliation into non-overlapping hyperplanes of frame-relative simultaneity. The latter can be under-stood as frame-relative moments of time. In the scenario depicted in Figure 10, points *p* and *q* are simultaneous relative to frame F, while *p* is later than *q* relative to frame F′.

A persisting material object can be described as having a property, such as a shape, at a frame-relative moment, t^F, for some frame F. The following scenario concerning an object's shape is a familiar consequence of relativity theory. Suppose that *o* is spherical at each moment of its life in frame F. Relative to a different frame, F′, *o* is not spherical throughout its life, but rather oblong. This is an instance of relativistic change. What does such change consist in?

It is compelling to understand relativistic change in shape as a perspectival phenomenon (Balashov, 2010, ch. 8; Sattig, 2015, ch. 8). In the case of *o* just

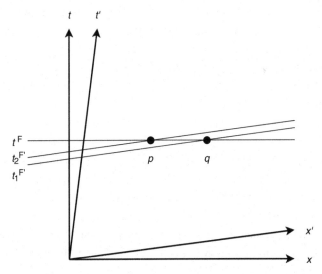

Figure 10 Temporal distances relative to inertial reference frames

sketched, there is an invariant geometrically four-dimensional shape that is the common ground of both the three-dimensional spherical shape that o has in F and the three-dimensional oblong shape that o has in F′. The different three-dimensional shapes at various frame-relative moments are all derived from one absolute four-dimensional shape. Let us call this the *perspectival account* of relativistic change. Perdurantism smoothly combines with this account. A perduring continuant, such as o, exactly occupies a unique four-dimensional region of spacetime. This is o's path. The shape of o at a frame-relative moment, t^F, is just the absolute shape of the region that is the intersection of o's path and t^F. Thus, as Yuri Balashov puts it, 'different 3D shapes are cross-sections of a single 4D object' (2010, pp. 202–3).

Can endurantists incorporate the perspectival account of relativistic change as well? Since enduring continuants lack an invariant exact location in space-time – they are multi-located in spacetime – the perspectival account might appear out of their reach. However, if enduring continuants have an invariant four-dimensional path, then the perspectival account can be sustained, even though a continuant does not exactly occupy its path. The key idea is that the different three-dimensional shapes of an enduring continuant are just cross-sections of its four-dimensional path.[37]

This strategy does not succeed. The main obstacle is that enduring continuants do not generally have invariant four-dimensional paths. Let us focus on the version of the endurantist package, according to which continuants are structured objects. Now consider the following counterexample (Sattig, 2015, pp. 226–7). A plurality of point-particles become arranged chair-wise very abruptly, at a moment t_1^F, for some frame F, and lose their chair-wise arrangement equally abruptly, say in an explosion, at t_2^F. As a consequence, a chair comes into existence at t_1^F and goes out of existence at t_2^F. Given that the chair is a structured object, it is natural to hold that it is a chair essentially. It has a chair structure with slots filled by the mentioned particles at all moments at which it exists in F. The path of the chair in F traced out by its parts is illustrated in the left half of Figure 11.

In the rest frame of the chair, F, the explosion and mutual separation of the particles occur simultaneously. In another frame, F′, associated with objects moving at a high speed relative to the chair, the explosion and mutual separation of the particles occur gradually. In F′, the chair loses its micro-parts one by one. Since the continuant is a chair essentially, it goes out of existence as the chair-wise arrangement of its parts breaks up. Similarly, the chair does not come into existence until the particles enter a chair-wise arrangement. As a result, the chair's path in F′ differs from its path in F, as illustrated in Figure 11. If the chair had the

---

[37] See Gilmore, 2008, for details and references.

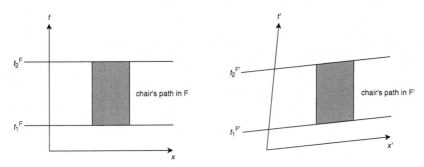

Figure 11 Endurance and relativity

same path in F′ as it has in F, it would come into existence before its micro-parts attain a chair-wise arrangement, and it would go out of existence after its micro-parts lose their chair-wise arrangement. Since this is impossible for a structured chair, the chair lacks an invariant four-dimensional path. Hence, the mentioned strategy of incorporating the perspectival account of relativistic change cannot be employed by endurantists who view continuants as structured.[38]

Since the perspectival account of relativistic change is prima facie compelling, perdurantists look like the clear winners in this debate. But the situation is more complicated. Notice first that the elegant perspectival account has a dark side. Assume perdurantism and suppose that a chair comes into and goes out of existence in the circumstances described previously, such that it persists from t_1^F to t_2^F, as before. Now suppose that in another frame, F′, there is a moment, $t^{F'}$, that overlaps with the chair's invariant path in a single spacetime point, as illustrated in Figure 12 (cf. Gilmore, 2006, p. 212). Since a perduring chair is not chair-shaped essentially, this scenario is consistent with the chair's nature. However, the result that our chair shrinks to a point in F′ clashes violently with the manifest image. Common sense assigns ordinary objects persistence conditions that govern how much the objects can change. And what could be more obvious, pre-theoretically, than that no chair can shrink to a point? Note here that in order to respect intuitive persistence conditions, the metaphysician need not view them as being encoded in the nature of objects. For the intuitive persistence conditions of objects may just have their source in the sortal concepts that apply to unstructured objects.[39] The upshot is

---

[38] Nor can it be employed by friends of unstructured endurers, since the latter cannot change in parts at all. But the chair would have to undergo radical mereological change, if it had the same path in F′ as in F.

[39] Similarly, Lewis' modal counterpart-theory (1986, ch. 4) lets possibilities for unstructured objects be determined by sortal concepts under which these objects fall.

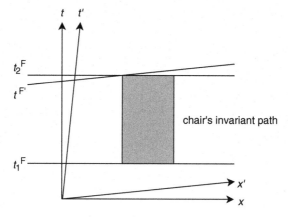

Figure 12 The point-shaped chair

that, by our ordinary concept of being a chair, chairs cannot shrink to a point, and hence the perduring whole in our example is not a chair, contrary to what was assumed at the outset.

Perdurantists might strike back with a simple reply. The perspectival account of relativistic shapes, they might claim, is strongly suggested by the standard interpretation of the *special theory of relativity* (STR). And when physics clashes with common sense, physics wins. So, once enlightened by physics, it is easy to live with the result that chairs can be point-shaped.

This reply is short-sighted. For there is reason to doubt that the perspectival account is strongly suggested by STR. At the centre of STR stand certain laws of nature that govern relations between frame-relative facts. The *Lorentz transformations* specify links between spatial and temporal distance-relations between points and regions in different reference frames. Consider points p and q. They have different spatial and temporal distances in different frames. On the standard interpretation of STR, the different spatial and temporal distances between p and q in different frames all derive from the same invariant spacetime interval between p and q. This interval is 'divided' into different spatial and temporal components in different frames, in a way that explains the Lorentz transformations. This is the gist of STR's take on spatial and temporal variation between inertial frames.

This familiar account of correlations between frame-relative facts applies to relativistic shapes of material objects in the following way. An object o's shape at a frame-relative moment, t^F, for any t in any F, is grounded in the spatial distance-relations among o's micro-parts, the xs, at t^F. Moreover, the xs inherit these spatial distance-relations at t^F from the spatial and temporal distance-relations among the spacetime points occupied by the xs at t^F. Finally, the latter points' distance-relations derive from the invariant spacetime intervals among these points. This is how, according to STR (given minimal assumptions about location), invariant spacetime intervals between the xs ground different spatial and temporal distance-relations among the xs in different frames. However, STR has nothing to say about whether the xs, which were assumed to be parts of o at t^F, are also parts of o in other reference frames. Accordingly, STR has nothing to say about whether o has different micro-parts in different frames, and hence has nothing to say about whether o has different four-dimensional paths in these frames. Facts of parthood, on which an object's path in a frame depends, are not the business of relativity theory in physics. STR is thus silent on whether a continuant has an invariant path or not. Since the existence of such an invariant path is central to the perspectival account of relativistic shapes, the perspectival account is not directly mandated by STR. The account is, rather, a substantial metaphysical addition to STR.

To conclude, while the perdurantists' perspectival account of relativistic change is, undoubtedly, the most elegant metaphysical addition to STR, endurantists retain some room to manoeuver. Prima facie, the perspectival account's clash with the manifest image speaks against the perdurantist approach to relativistic change. And since the perspectival account is not strongly supported by STR, the account's violation of common sense cannot be downplayed easily.[40]

3 Paradox

We have a philosophical paradox, or a puzzle, when several pre-philosophically innocuous assumptions are incompatible. This section is about a range of paradoxes concerning material objects. These paradoxes bring to the fore apparent inconsistencies in the manifest image of objects. Paradoxes of coincidence are the subject of Section 3.1. Paradoxes of fission are the subjects of Section 3.2. And the problem of the many is the subject of Section 3.3.

3.1 Paradoxes of Coincidence

How many material objects can fit into a spatial region at a time? Intuitively, the right answer is 'one'. The exact location of non-identical objects at the same place at the same moment would amount to overcrowding. Let us say that an object, o, and an object, o', *coincide* at a moment t just in case o and o' exactly occupy the same spatial region at t.[41] The following *anti-coincidence principle*

---

[40] See Sattig, 2015, ch. 8, for an upgrade of the perdurantists' perspectival account, which affords a reconciliation with the manifest image of objects.

[41] This is a widely used term. 'Co-location' would be suitable as well. Some reserve the term 'coincidence' for mereological coincidence. For o and o' to coincide at t in this sense is for o and o' to have the same parts at t.

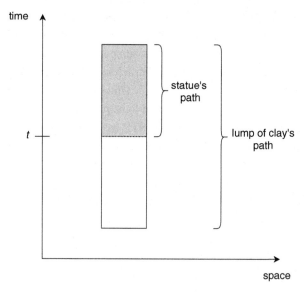

Figure 13 The statue and the lump of clay

(AC) seems to feature as a rule in the manifest image of objects: for any ordinary objects, *o* and *o′*, and any moment *t*, if *o* coincides with *o′* at *t*, then *o* is identical with *o′*. Yet AC has a number of prima facie compelling counterexamples, giving rise to various paradoxes of coincidence. I shall focus on four cases.

First, an artisan moulds a statue from a lump of clay. When the process is completed, at moment *t*, there is a statue and a lump of clay. While the lump existed before the artisan went to work, the statue did not. Thus, the statue and the lump are non-identical. Yet the statue and the lump exactly occupy the same spatial regions, and hence they coincide, after *t*. This case is illustrated in Figure 13.

Second, Tibbles is a cat and Tib is a lump of feline tissue consisting of all of Tibbles except for her tail. They are non-identical objects, since they differ in their parts. Now, suppose that Tibbles loses her tail at *t*. Since a cat can survive the loss of certain parts, such as tails, Tibbles survives. Moreover, since nothing happens to Tib apart from having something external detached from it, Tib survives as well. Hence, Tibbles and Tib coincide after *t*, as illustrated in Figure 14.[42]

Third, a chair is built from a piece of wood. The chair has four legs and is functionally defective. The piece of wood, by contrast, does not have any legs and is not defective. Hence, the chair and the piece of wood coincide (Sattig,

---

[42] See Geach, 1980, and Wiggins, 1967.

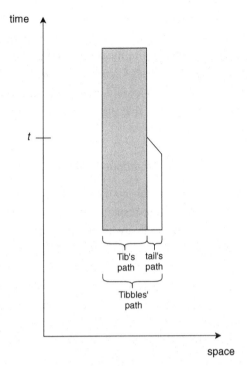

Figure 14 Tibbles and Tib

2015, p. 78). Notice that this case, unlike the first two, just appeals to differences between two objects at the moment of their coincide.[43]

Fourth, suppose that a piece of paper and a paper aeroplane are created and destroyed at the same moments, such that the piece of paper and the paper plane coincide throughout their lives. Since the objects have the same physical properties and the same parts throughout their lives, the reasons for judgements of non-identity that apply in previous cases do not apply here. Nevertheless, there are good reasons for judging the piece of paper and the paper plane to be non-identical, for they have different modal properties: the piece of paper could survive being flattened, while the paper plane could not. Hence, we have a case of distinct permanent coincidents.[44]

Each of these cases is a counterexample to AC, according to which no distinct ordinary objects can coincide at any moment. In what follows, I shall review a range of responses to these paradoxes. Most responses are *incompatibilist*, in virtue of viewing the paradoxes as uncovering a genuine inconsistency in the manifest image and rejecting one or more of the compelling

---

[43] See Fine, 2003, for more examples of this sort.   [44] Compare Gibbard, 1975.

premises that unleash the paradoxes. Resolving the apparent conflict between AC and the various cases of distinct coincidents is usually thought to require a choice between denying the plausibility of the cases and rejecting AC – that is, a choice between *monism* and *pluralism* about coincidence. I shall begin with two monist responses, then consider two pluralist ones, and finally sketch a *compatibilist* manoeuver that attempts to reconcile the cases with AC.

3.1.1 Monism about Coincidence

Monists accept AC and reject one or more of the assumptions that govern the counterexamples. A simple monist response to the first case – the *phasalist response* (Jubien, 2001)[45] – denies that when the lump of clay acquires a statue shape a new object comes into existence. Rather, so the response, the same object that falls only under the sortal concept *lump of clay* before *t* falls under the sortal concept *statue* as well as *lump of clay* after *t*. The sortal *statue* is here treated as a *phase sortal* that can apply to an object at some but not all moments of its existence. The whole scenario thus contains but a single ordinary object, and hence AC is preserved. The key phasalist move, as I understand it, is to claim that the apparent non-identity of the statue and the lump of clay is an illusion induced by a difference in sortal concepts.

While the phasalist response defuses the first case elegantly, its scope is severely limited. For the apparent non-identity of Tibbles and Tib in the second case cannot be explained away in this fashion. The phasalist's diagnosis of the first case is that we naively count the coinciding objects as two objects because different sortal concepts apply to them. Since, according to the phasalist, one of the sortals is a phase sortal, this reasoning is faulty. This type of diagnosis does not apply to the second case. For here we count the coinciding objects, Tibbles and Tib, as two objects because they have different parts (at a moment prior to their coincidence), not because different sortal concepts apply to them.

A monist response with a wider scope of application is the *dominant-sorts response* (Burke, 1994; Rea, 2000). While an ordinary object may fall under different sortal concepts, or belong to different kinds, only one of them is dominant. The dominant sortal of the object is the one that determines the object's persistence conditions. In application to the first case, the key move is to cut down on the number of artefacts present at each moment by rejecting the seemingly innocuous assumption that the lump of clay making up the statue after *t* is identical with the lump of clay before *t*. According to this response,

---

[45] The term 'phasalism' is due to Korman (2015, p. 204).

moulding a lump of clay into a statue destroys the lump since this process causes a transition from one dominant sortal – namely, *lump* – to another dominant sortal – namely, *statue*. Similarly, the account rejects the assumption of the second case that Tib, the lump of tissue, survives the removal of Tibbles' tail, although this is a removal of a mere external attachment of Tib. Notice, finally, that since this response's key to the paradoxes concerns change with respect to the dominance-status of sortal concepts, or kinds, it has nothing to say about the third case, which involves no change at all.[46]

3.1.2 Pluralism about Coincidence

Pluralists accept at least some of the cases of distinct coincidents but reject AC. The star among the pluralist responses is the perdurantist account of coincidence as *temporal overlap* (Lewis, 1983a). According to perdurantism (Section 2.1), the statue and the lump of clay exactly occupy different temporally extended spacetime regions (illustrated in Figure 13) and hence are nonidentical. Moreover, an object exactly occupies a spatial region, r, at t by having a temporal part at t, which exactly occupies r simpliciter. Thus, the perdurantist is in a position to say that the statue and the lump coincide after t, in virtue of sharing temporal parts after t. Similarly, Tibbles and Tib coincide after t by sharing temporal parts after t. Given that spatial location at a moment is grounded in spatial location simpliciter, no spatial region is occupied by more than one object simpliciter. Perdurantists do not simply reject AC. They present the principle in a different light. They plead that we should not worry about whether distinct ordinary objects exactly occupy the same region at the same time, tout court. What we should worry about instead is whether distinct ordinary objects exactly occupy the same region at the same time, in the most basic sense of 'occupation'. In other words, coincidence of distinct objects is only repugnant when it goes metaphysically deep. The temporal-overlap response shows that deep down, where objects are described in terms of occupation, or location, simpliciter, there are no distinct coincidents. Hence, we can live with the rejection of AC and the resulting rift in the manifest image.

The third case marks a limitation of the temporal-overlap response. Since sharing a temporal part at t entails sharing all spatial parts at t, the perdurantist is unable to capture the mereological difference between the chair and the piece of wood. This does not come as a surprise, in light of the discussion of Section 1.3. Perdurantists typically view ordinary objects as unstructured, whereas, pre-philosophically, parthood is kind-sensitive and ordinary objects are structured.

---

[46] The dominant-sorts view also struggles with cases of same-kind coincidence; see Fine, 2000.

The fourth case also presents a situation quite different from the first and the second. Here, the piece of paper and the paper plane coincide permanently. Since they share all of their temporal parts, standard perdurantists view them as being the same object. Consequently, they face the challenge of accounting for the difference in modal properties of the piece of paper and the paper plane. We have two modal profiles but only one object. If an object has its modal profile absolutely, then this combination is unstable. If, by contrast, an object has a modal profile relative to a way of thinking about the object, then one object may have different modal profiles relative to different ways of thinking about it. This is how Lewis (1983b, 1986, sect. 4.5) famously proposed to handle cases such as the fourth one. Lewis' account goes roughly as follows. One object falls under the sortal concept *piece of paper* and also under the sortal concept *paper plane*. These two sortals determine different *counterpart relations* between our object and non-identical objects in other possible worlds. As the case was introduced, the piece of paper could survive flattening, while the paper plane could not. On Lewis' account of modal properties of objects, this claim is correct because our object has piece-of-paper-counterparts that are flat, while the same object lacks paper-plane-counterparts that are flat. Notice that the Lewisian package of perdurantism and modal counterpart-theory is not uniformly pluralist. The first and second cases receive a pluralist treatment, while the third and fourth receive a monist treatment.

Many endurantists have endorsed a pluralism of a very different shape. Let us focus on the first case. The statue and the lump of clay are non-identical enduring objects that coincide at *t*. Therefore, AC is false. How dramatic is the breakdown of this platitude of common sense? As we know by now, endurantism is typically motivated by how well it plays with common sense. With this in mind, the breakdown of AC threatens to tarnish endurantism's image considerably. Can they control the damage? We have seen how perdurantists do it. That distinct ordinary objects coincide at a moment does not go deep. For occupation at a moment derives from occupation simpliciter. And there are no objects that coincide simpliciter. Endurantist damage control works differently. The key, according to many endurantists, is the relation of *constitution* among non-identical things: when one thing constitutes another, the latter derives its very being from the former. The lump of clay is thought to constitute the statue, and hence the statue derives its being from the lump.[47] With the notion of constitution at their disposal, endurantists can adduce their own reason of why the coincidence of distinct objects does not run deep. The endurantist

---

[47] For discussion of the nature of constitution, see Baker, 2000, 2007; Koslicki, 2008; Kovacs, 2020; Thomson, 1998.

constitutionalist's standard account of why this is so goes roughly as follows. The fact that the statue exactly occupies a spatial region, *r*, at *t* is explained by the fact that the statue is constituted by a lump of clay that exactly occupies *r* at *t*. On this picture, the statue and the lump do not crowd each other out, since they do not inhabit the same 'level of reality'. Since the statue inherits its being from the lump's being, at the level of reality at which we find the lump we will not find the statue as well. This response applies straightforwardly to all four cases. In the second case, Tib constitutes Tibbles after *t*. In the third case, the piece of wood constitutes the chair at the moment under consideration. And in the fourth case, the piece of paper constitutes the paper plane throughout the lives of both objects.

While this is an impressive entrance, worries arise quickly as the details of the constitutionalist account are brought into focus. Suppose that a block of wood, B, presently constitutes a table, T. Being a typical table, T could be made of a different material than the material it is actually made of. T is actually made of wood but could be made of metal instead. (Imagine that T's wooden parts were gradually replaced by metal parts.) If T derives its very being from B, as constitutionalists claim, then we should expect that the nature of B contributes to the nature of T. At least, this is something essentialists about objects should expect. And constitutionalists are usually essentialists. Assume, plausibly, that B is essentially a block of wood. Since T derives its being from B, T is essentially made of wood as well, and hence T could not be made of metal instead. This contradicts our initial assumption. Here is a different formulation of the objection. Given that tablehood is the unique essential kind of T, all non-trivial essential properties of T must be relevant to being a table. But being made of wood, rather than of metal or plastic, is not relevant to being a table. Being a table is a functional kind.[48]

I shall conclude my review of pluralism about coincidence with a look at a widely discussed challenge for endurantist constitutionalism that arises specifically in the fourth case. The piece of paper and the paper plane differ in their modal profile. For instance, the former can survive flattening, while the latter cannot. What do these possibilities for an object – these possibilities *de re* – consist in? What grounds them? We looked at several questions of this type in previous sections. Here, as in other domains, a primitivist denial of the need for an explanation is one option. Those who, instead, rise to the

---

[48] The technical notion of constitution is to be distinguished from a more intuitive notion that is sometimes invoked in introductory settings. For instance, 'problems of constitution' are often introduced as questions concerning how the statue is related to the lump of clay that constitutes the statue. This use of the term 'constitution' is best understood in terms of causation: what is the metaphysical relationship between the statue and the lump of clay that was involved in the creation of the statue? This intuitive, causal understanding might explain the wide appeal of constitution-talk, but it does not help with the paradoxes of coincidence.

explanatory challenge might be inclined to answer as follows: an object's kind determines its possibilities. Being a piece of paper is compatible with having a flat shape, while being a paper plane is incompatible with having a flat shape. So, the *de re* modal difference between our two objects has its source in the fact that one is a paper plane and not a piece of paper, while the other is a piece of paper and not a paper plane. Surely, however, the properties of being a piece of paper and of being a paper plane are not fundamental properties of any object. An object is a piece of paper because it has certain more basic properties and relations. Likewise for an object's being a paper plane. In our case of permanent coincidents, what grounds the suggested difference in kind-membership, given that the two objects seem to share all of their non-modal properties and relations throughout their lives? This is known as the *grounding problem*.[49]

The most straightforward response to this problem is outlined hereafter (Baker, 2000). To begin with, the two objects do not differ in kind, contrary to the initial proposal. Since they are indiscernible with respect to their non-modal properties and relations, and since ordinary kinds are not fundamental properties, each object is a piece of paper and a paper plane. However, only one of the two is a piece of paper essentially, while the other is a paper plane essentially. And this difference in essential kinds – a difference in the objects' nature – is the source of their modal difference. As essentialists commonly hold, an object's having a given property essentially is a fundamental fact, even if an object's just having this property is a derivative fact. Is this response ad hoc? That is, does the notion of an essential kind serve no other purpose than to solve the grounding problem? No. As discussed in Section 1.3, the very idea of a structured object plausibly builds upon the notion of an essential kind.[50]

3.1.3 Compatibilism about Coincidence

Compatibilists claim that AC and the various cases, when they are understood properly, are not in tension. The main reason for seeking such a resolution is simple. If the manifest image really takes centre stage in the study of objects, we had better strive for an account that makes the manifest image consistent. A recent compatibilist response to the paradoxes of coincidence is offered by *perspectivalism* (Sattig, 2015, ch. 3). The key idea, roughly, is that we conceive of ordinary objects differently in different contexts. On the *sortal-sensitive* conception, we represent ordinary objects in ways that are sensitive to the

---

[49] For discussion, see Baker, 2000; Bennett, 2004; deRosset, 2011; Fine, 2008; Heller, 1991; Rea, 1997; Saenz, 2015; Sattig, 2015; Sutton, 2012; Zimmerman, 1995.

[50] Compare the essentialist response to the problem of collapse discussed in Section 2.2.

kinds to which the objects belong. On the *sortal-abstract* conception, we represent ordinary objects in a primarily spatiotemporal way that abstracts from which kinds the objects belong to. The descriptions of specific non-identical ordinary objects as coinciding in our four cases exhibit the sortal-sensitive conception. The sweeping rejection of the possibility of non-identical coincidents, by contrast, exhibits the sortal-abstract perspective. Thus, from the sortal-sensitive perspective, the world is crowded with distinct coincidents, whereas from the sortal-abstract perspective, no distinct coincidents are to be found anywhere.

Perspectivalism about coincidence permits various metaphysical foundations. Here is my preferred candidate, to be sketched briefly in application to the first case. There is, in this scenario, a persisting unstructured material object, *a*. I shall leave open whether it endures or perdures. The account is compatible with each approach to the persistence of *a*. At every moment of its life, *a* is in some *lump-of-clay-state*, where each of these complex states realizes the kind *lump of clay*. The conjunction of all of these states is *a*'s *lump-of-clay-path*. From moment *t* onwards, *a* is also in a range of *statue-states*, each of which realizes the kind *statue*. The conjunction of all of these is *a*'s *statue-path*. The two *K-paths*, for different kinds K, are non-identical.[51] Now, the (unstructured) sum of *a* and its lump-of-clay-path is our lump of clay, whereas the sum of *a* and its statue-path is our statue. Given this metaphysical account of ordinary objects as compounds of an unstructured material object and a K-path of that object, for some kind K, we are in a position to say that judgements about an ordinary object from the sortal-sensitive perspective are made true by the object's component K-path, whereas judgements from the sortal-abstract perspective are made true by the object's component material object. From the sortal-sensitive perspective, the statue and the lump are non-identical, coinciding objects, since they have different K-paths as components. But from the sortal-abstract perspective, the statue and the lump are one and the same object, and hence AC is preserved, since they share their component material object.[52]

3.2 Paradoxes of Fission

Suppose that a person P's brain is implanted into a new head and fully connected. The post-operation person remembers P's past experiences and shares her personality traits. In short, the post-operation person is *psychologically continuous* with P. Is the post-operation person identical with P? Does

---

[51] K-paths of material objects are to be distinguished from four-dimensional paths of objects in spacetime (see Section 2.1).

[52] For details, see Sattig, 2010, 2015, ch. 1.

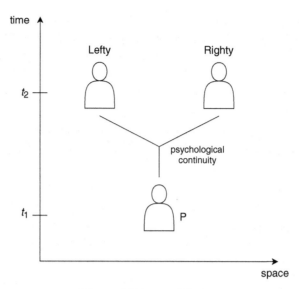

Figure 15 Personal fission

P survive the operation? Many share the intuition that identity obtains, and hence that P survives. Indeed, when the case is described from the subjective point of view of the post-operation person, it is hard to resist the judgement that she is P, since her mental life before the operation just is P's.

Now consider a modification of this case. Suppose that the corpus callosum connecting the two hemispheres of P's brain is severed. This is a well-known surgical procedure for treating epilepsy, known as corpus callosotomy. Suppose, further, that each hemisphere is then trained to take over the tasks that were previously performed by its neighbour. Callosotomies revealed that this is possible. Suppose, finally, that the hemispheres are removed and each is implanted in a different head. Each hemisphere is fully connected and comes to function in its new skull just as it used to function in the old one. As a result, there are persons, Lefty and Righty, who are psychologically continuous with P in every way. This is a case of *personal fission*.[53] It is illustrated in Figure 15.

The fate of P in the non-branching case was intuitively clear: P survives. But what happens to P in the branching case? Since P is linked to Lefty and Righty in the same way, it cannot be the case that P is identical with one rather than the other. Three answers come to mind. First, P survives twice over, and hence Lefty and Righty are one and the same person. The latter exactly occupies different spatial

[53] See Parfit, 1984; Shoemaker, 1963; Williams, 1956. A related thought experiment lets a line of psychological continuity branch out by double transfer of P's brain-states to two different brains (Johnston, 1987).

regions after the operation, at t_2. This response is simple but outrageous, since it violates a platitude of common sense: ordinary objects are confined to a single region at a time. Let us call this platitude the *anti-bilocation principle* (AB).

Second, P was not alone before the operation (Lewis, 1983a). Fission does not divide one person. It separates distinct persons. Thus, Lefty and Righty are non-identical persons that coincide before the operation, at t_1. This description is also hard to accept. For it clashes with another platitude of common sense, with which we are familiar already, namely, AC (see Section 3.1).

Third, P dies in the operation, and hence P, Lefty, and Righty are non-identical persons. Given that P survives when she is psychologically continuous with just one person that exists at t_2 – this is the non-branching case – the question arises as to why P goes out of existence when she is psychologically continuous with two persons that exist at t_2. The standard response is that the persistence of persons is non-local (Nozick, 1981). Whether P is identical with Lefty does not just depend on how P and Lefty are connected. It also depends on whether there are other strong candidates for identity with P, such as Righty. Since Lefty and Righty are equally strong candidates for identity with P, P is identical with neither. The third description of the outcome of personal fission is just as repugnant as the other two. For here Lefty comes into existence at t_2 because Righty is around at t_2 (and vice versa). This clashes with the common-sense principle that no ordinary object comes into or goes out of existence by purely extrinsic causes. I shall call this the *anti-extrinsicness principle* (AE).

The foregoing three descriptions of what happens to P in the fission case are the most salient ones. Each of them is based on the intuitively plausible assumption that a person goes where its mental life goes. Moreover, each description is incompatible with some platitude of common sense. This is the *paradox of personal fission*.

3.2.1 Incompatibilism about Fission

Incompatibilists reject the initial assumption that a person goes where its mental life goes – that psychological continuity grounds personal persistence – or they reject at least one of the platitudes of common sense. Let us consider the two approaches in turn.

The view that the persistence of persons is grounded in psychological continuity, which licenses the opening assumption of the fission paradox, is the most popular position in the venerable debate on personal persistence, or personal identity over time.[54] Among incompatibilists of the first type, it is common to reject this view in favour of some account of personal persistence in

---

[54] This view is typically attributed to John Locke, 1690/1975.

terms of non-psychological facts about persons. They hold that a person does not necessarily go where its mental life goes. Many of these incompatibilists believe that a person like us is identical with a human organism, and hence that the person goes where the organism goes. This response will shut down fission paradoxes only if branching cases are confined to persons. It is far from clear, however, whether this is the case. If it is possible for lines of biological continuity to branch out, then a paradox of organism fission with an analogous layout arises. It has been suggested that the division of amoeba is an actual case of biological fission. Furthermore, there are many cases of dividing artefacts, such as the famous case of the Ship of Theseus.[55]

According to incompatibilists of the second type, fission reveals that persons really can be bilocated or really can coincide or really can go out of existence by purely extrinsic causes. This type of approach may be accompanied by a recipe for downplaying deviance from the manifest image, such as the recipes we encountered in Section 3.1.

Perdurantism offers the most elegant version of this response. As regards the first description of personal fission, perdurantists who adopt it can point out that bilocation does not go metaphysically deep. There are, fundamentally, no bilocated objects, since no temporal part of a person has more than one exact spatial location simpliciter. That is, at the metaphysical 'level' at which objects are described in terms of location simpliciter, there are no bilocated objects. And since we should only worry about deep bilocation, we can live with the rejection of AB in fission cases.

As regards the second description, there is, fundamentally, no coincidence of distinct objects, since at any spatial region at any time – that is, at any spacetime region – at most one instantaneous stage is located simpliciter. Since we should only worry about deep coincidence, we can live with the rejection of AC in fission cases.

As regards the third description of fission, no object comes into or goes out of existence by purely extrinsic causes, fundamentally speaking. This is so, because no object really comes into or goes out of existence in the first place. Ordinary talk of objects coming into and going out of existence is made true by facts concerning which collections of absolutely, atemporally existing instantaneous stages are qualitatively related in which ways. Since we should only worry about whether non-local creation or destruction of objects occurs at the fundamental 'level' of reality, we can live with the rejection of AE in fission cases.[56]

---

[55] While the Ship of Theseus presents a paradox of the same type as the fission paradox, the persistence of artefacts raises its own widely discussed challenges.
[56] Compare Sider's non-locality-response to the collapse problem in Section 2.2.

3.2.2 Compatibilism about Fission

The stage view (introduced in Section 2.1) offers a widely recognized compatibilist response to fission paradoxes (Sider, 2001, sect. 5.8). According to this position, the case of personal fission contains, inter alia, the following three instantaneous stages: a stage, a, that only exists at t_1 and two stages, b and c, that only exist at t_2, where a and b as well as a and c are linked by the temporal counterpart relation for persons. Assuming that a is a person, there is, at t_1, exactly one, uniquely located person. This person persists until t_2 along local lines of psychological continuity, in virtue of having both b and c as temporal counterparts. And yet at t_2, there are exactly two, uniquely located persons, namely, b and c. This description of personal fission presupposes that statements of personal persistence are made true by relations of psychological continuity among stages, and it is compatible with the three platitudes of common sense.

This way out comes at a significant cost. How many persons are involved in the process of double-hemisphere transplant? This question exhibits a cross-temporal attitude towards the case, which is perfectly common for ordinary thinkers. Sensible answers to the cross-temporal question are 'one person', 'two persons', and 'three persons'. The stage view's answer, by contrast, is 'so many persons that it is practically impossible to count them all'. For each instantaneous stage involved in our scenario is a person. That is the dark side of the stage view.

The stage view employs the notion of absolute identity only. An alternative compatibilist approach to fission paradoxes rejects this notion in favour of irreducibly temporally relativized identity (Gallois, 2003; Langford & Ramachandran, 2013). Lefty and Righty are non-identical at t_2. Moreover, Lefty already exists at t_1, and so does Righty. But at t_1, Lefty and Righty are identical. The price of this solution to the paradoxes of fission is deviance from the standard concept of identity. Few metaphysicians have been willing to go this far.

Another compatibilist resolution is offered by perspectivalism (introduced in Section 3.1; Sattig, 2015, ch. 4). The basic idea, details aside, is the following. Ordinary thinkers conceive of persons and other ordinary objects from different conceptual perspectives. The three descriptions of the outcome of fission exhibit the sortal-sensitive perspective, privileging psychological properties that realize the kind *person*. The platitudes of common sense, on the other hand, exhibit the sortal-abstract perspective, privileging spatiotemporal properties shared by all ordinary objects. The descriptions and principles, exhibiting different perspectives, are compatible because they are made true by different metaphysical components of persons. While this approach does not determine which description of the outcome of personal fission is the correct one, it prevents each description from tearing apart the manifest image of objects.

3.3 The Problem of the Many

Indeterminate boundaries of ordinary objects raise the *problem of the many* (Geach, 1980; Unger, 1980; Weatherson, 2016). Suppose that mountain M is the sole mountain on an open plain. M is composed of rocks. For many rocks on M's surface, it is unclear whether they are parts of M. M seems to be *mereologically indeterminate*. So, there are many ways of drawing the mountain's boundary. Assuming that each boundary we draw corresponds to an aggregate of rocks, each of these aggregates is a candidate to be the mountain on the plain, M. It does not seem possible to single out one of the candidates as M, since each seems to be an equally good candidate to be the mountain. None of them is special. But if each of them is a mountain, then there are many mountains on the plain. And if none of them is a mountain, then there is no mountain on the plain. Either way, it is not the case that there is one mountain on the plain, contrary to what we expected.[57]

The task presented by this problem is to explain what mereological indeterminacy of ordinary objects consists in, while sustaining our familiar practice of counting these objects. The most widely discussed solution to the problem of the many is the *supervaluationist account*. To begin with, the latter builds upon standard *supervaluationism*, the dominant brand of linguistic theory of indeterminacy (Fine, 1975; Lewis, 1993; see Section 1.2). To the supervaluationist, indeterminacy arises as a result of semantic imprecision. An expression is semantically imprecise when its meaning can be precisified in different ways that are consistent with speakers' use of the expression. In the case of M, mereological indeterminacy arises from imprecision in how we refer to objects. There is a cluster of massively overlapping aggregates of rocks with different precise decompositions, such that no candidate is the referent of 'M', but each is a candidate to be designated by 'M', as illustrated in Figure 16.

Given these assumptions, it is indeterminate whether M has rock *r* as a part, because some candidate referents of 'M' have *r* as a part, while other candidate referents lack *r* as a part. On this account, the indeterminacy is *de dicto*: it is indeterminate whether a certain description of the world is true, while the world itself is precise.

While these considerations take care of the mereological indeterminacy of M, the supervaluationist has yet to explain why there is exactly one mountain on the plain. She cannot recognize each of the candidate referents of 'M' as being

---

[57] This sketch of the problem of the many is adapted from Sattig, 2015, ch. 7.

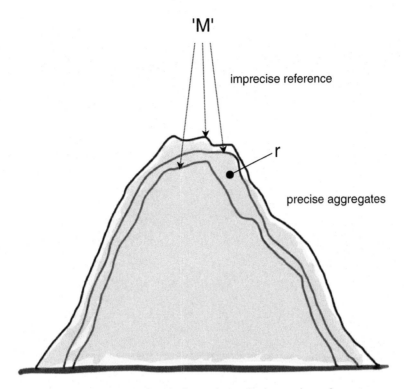

Figure 16 Mereological indeterminacy by imprecise reference

a mountain. For then there are many mountains. What to do? The supervaluationist can offer the following popular response. Not only 'M' is semantically imprecise. The sortal term *mountain* is imprecise as well. Each of the many candidates for being a mountain is neither clearly a mountain nor clearly not a mountain. It is unclear whether the sortal term applies to any of them. And yet it is true that there is exactly one mountain on the plain. The key move in securing this result is to declare that on each admissible precisification of the sortal term *mountain* the latter applies to exactly one of the aggregates on the plain. While none of these aggregates is the one mountain on the plain, it is still determinately true that there is one mountain on the plain (McGee & McLaughlin, 2000).

This response to the problem of the many is ingenious but quite artificial. One cannot help wondering how each admissible precisification of *mountain* manages to single out exactly one aggregate on the plain. For this to work, we expect each precisification of the sortal to specify a property or cluster of properties that determines what makes an object a mountain, and that only one of the candidates has. But this is a requirement the precisifications probably cannot satisfy.

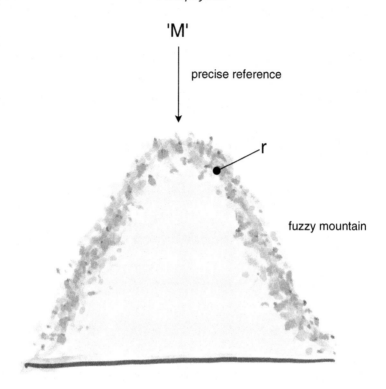

Figure 17 Mereological indeterminacy by imprecise objects

Since the overlapping candidates may differ only minutely, by a rock or two, it seems that any such property (or property cluster) would apply to several of the candidates, making it false that there is one mountain on the plain. Alternatively, the property would fail to apply to any or sufficiently many aggregates of rocks elsewhere, making it false that there are a few thousand mountains in Switzerland. This is one of a number of challenges for those who locate the source of the problem of the many in how we represent the world.[58]

One route around these obstacles is to construe the name 'M' as referring precisely to an imprecise, or fuzzy, object, as illustrated in Figure 17. The proposal is that there is one composite on the plain that falls under the sortal *mountain*, and that this object is mereologically indeterminate *de re*. The latter is a form of metaphysical indeterminacy, which is entirely independent of how we represent the world (compare Section 1.2).

Three questions about this proposal arise immediately. First, what does metaphysical indeterminacy consist in? The standard view is to treat such

---

[58] See McKinnon, 2002; Sattig, 2015, sect. 7.1.

indeterminacy as fundamental, in the sense that facts about indeterminacy are not grounded in any more basic, indeterminacy-free facts.[59] One way to shed some light on fundamental metaphysical indeterminacy is to suggest that somehow reality itself has different precisifications. This idea has been developed by treating metaphysical indeterminacy as a kind of modality, which concerns multiple actualities, worlds that are precisificationally possible.[60] In this framework, mereological indeterminacy can be illuminated by supervaluating over the varying mereological profiles of a given object in different actual worlds. Thus, it is indeterminate of M – that is, indeterminate *de re* – whether it has *r* as a part because there is an actuality in which M has *r* as a part and another actuality in which M lacks *r* as a part. While this and other proposals have contributed to rendering metaphysical indeterminacy intelligible, few philosophers have taken the plunge and endorsed a picture of this type.

Second, even if it is accepted that M has different parts in different precisificational worlds – in different actualities – the question ensues as to what grounds this precisificational profile of M. This is a grounding problem reminiscent of the one encountered in Section 3.1. M needs to be treated as a structured object. Unstructured objects should be viewed as precise, since each part of an unstructured object is essential to it, and an object's nature remains constant across different precisificational worlds, just as it remains constant across different possible worlds. If so, which facts about M's form, or slot-structure, determine how M varies in mereological profile across different actualities?

Third, assuming that M is a fuzzy mountain, what grounds the fact that there is exactly one fuzzy mountain on the plain, rather than many? Explaining the mereological indeterminacy of M is one task. Explaining the sparsity of fuzzy mountains on the plain is a further task. Ambitious solutions to the problem of the many will tackle both tasks at once. But both are exceedingly difficult.

4 Existence

The discussions of the previous sections make certain framing assumptions about the existence of material objects. One assumption is that composite material objects exist. Another assumption is that the notion of existence in play in the various metaphysical debates about objects is the notion of existence championed by ontological realists. The aim of the remainder of this Element is to review some ways of resisting these assumptions. Section 4.1 will be

---

[59] See Sattig, 2015, sect. 7.3, for an account of mereological indeterminacy *de re* as nonfundamental.

[60] See Akiba, 2000; Barnes & Williams, 2011; Parsons, 2000. Some invoke the modal approach, in order to illuminate rather than to reduce metaphysical indeterminacy.

concerned with different considerations in support of mereological nihilism. Sections 4.2 and 4.3 will be concerned with reconceptualizations of the debate about the existence of composite material objects from the point of view of alternatives to standard ontological realism.

4.1 Mereological Nihilism, Experience, and Science

The debates reviewed in previous sections presuppose that there are composite material objects. It is time to question this presupposition. Why not adopt mereological nihilism instead? According to mereological nihilism, no composite things exist (see Section 1.1). The view is typically advertized as being the simplest view of composition and existence. Why is it simpler than mereological restrictivism and universalism? It is, firstly, *ontologically* simpler, in virtue of recognizing fewer objects. As we saw in the discussion of universalism and restrictivism (Section 1.2), however, ontological simplicity of a view on composition is not obviously a major virtue if composition is generative and wholes derive from their parts (or vice versa). It is, secondly, *ideologically* simpler, in virtue of getting by without a primitive notion of parthood. The reality described by mereological nihilism has a simpler fundamental structure (Sider, 2013, sect. 1). It is not just the case, according to nihilists, that composition never occurs. There is, they add, no fundamental relation of parthood to begin with.[61] So, what's not to like? I shall review two attempts of opposing nihilism as well as various challenges to these attempts on behalf of nihilists.

4.1.1 Experience

Composite objects feature in the manifest image. Many contemporary metaphysicians hold that a belief's being shared by most counts as support – perhaps as one factor among others – for the belief. Some of them seek to locate a source of our everyday object-beliefs and point to perceptual experiences as such a source – perhaps as one source among others. Suppose, then, that a subject, S, encounters a scene with a table-shaped arrangement of qualities and has a visual experience with the content that there is a table in front of her. Since it is reasonable to trust perceptual experience as a source of information about the world, S's table-experience gives her a prima facie reason to believe that there are tables, and hence to believe that mereological nihilism is false.

Nihilists have challenged the view of perceptual experience as a source of justification for beliefs about the existence of objects by arguing that SCQ is not

---

[61] If the main plus of mereological nihilism is the avoidance of primitive parthood then a viable reductive account of parthood would weaken nihilism. While some notion of parthood is usually taken as primitive, see Sattig, 2019, for a reductive proposal.

an empirical question. We are not, they claim, perceptually sensitive to the differences between the various answers to SCQ. Specifically, S's visual table-experience is not sensitive to the difference between the scenario containing some particles arranged tablewise but no table and the scenario containing a table in addition to the particles. Moreover, that S does in fact have this perceptual table-experience, despite the latter's insensitivity to facts of composition, can be explained by biological and cultural factors alone.[62] In short, perceptual experience does not teach us about the mereological structure of the world – we do not possess a perceptual composition-detector.

This way lies the madness of radical scepticism. So the anti-nihilist might respond. Perceptual experience cannot show us that we are not stuck in a computer simulation either. Yet most of us are convinced that simulation-based sceptical attacks are mistaken. Given how basic a source of information perceptual experience is, it is often considered more reasonable to reject the premises in a sceptical argument against the trustworthiness of these experiences, than to accept the argument's conclusion, even if we cannot pinpoint the wrong step on the way to this conclusion. This, accordingly, is the suggested recipe for moving past exotic computer-simulation possibilities that conflict with the contents of experience: don't take them too seriously! If the attack from mereological nihilism on the trustworthiness of our perceptual experiences is of the same type as simulation-based attacks, then the mentioned recipe instructs us to downplay the nihilist attack as well.

It is far from clear whether these attacks deserve the same treatment. It should be agreed that when perceptual experiences conflict with powerful scientific theories – say, just for illustration, with string theory – then this conflict must be taken very seriously. Prima facie justification by experience may, of course, be defeated or undermined by scientific evidence. On the other hand, when perceptual experiences conflict with radical simulation scenarios from science fiction, then this conflict need not be taken so seriously. Where on the spectrum from science fiction to string theory is mereological nihilism to be placed? Some say that mereological nihilism is closer to science fiction than to string theory. In comparison with viable scientific theories, they hold, metaphysical accounts of composition are cheap: they are formulated at an extremely high level of abstraction, answer to comparatively few constraints, and are supported by rather weak evidence, such as considerations of simplicity. Others say that mereological nihilism is closer to string theory than to science fiction. In contrast to computer-simulation stories, they hold, nihilism is a real option, a hypothesis taken seriously by many reasonable people, for which there is at

---

[62] See Merricks, 2001, ch. 3, for this sort of challenge.

least some positive evidence, and which we can expect to integrate well with our best scientific theories.[63] Wrapping up these sparse remarks, it is probably fair to say that the issue of the status of perceptual evidence in the metaphysics of composition is fuzzy and difficult to get under control.[64] Is there any clearer evidence to work with?

4.1.2 Science

Our best scientific theories refer to and quantify over composite objects of all sizes, from the nucleons of particle physics and the molecules of chemistry to the organisms of biology and the heavenly bodies of astronomy. Since it is rational to trust the verdicts of our best scientific theories, it is rational to believe that composites exist. Mereological nihilists have resisted this argument with a two-step manoeuvre (Rosen & Dorr, 2002, sect. 7). The first step is to point out that the assumption of scientific theories that there are composites is unquestioned and untested. Nihilist alternatives to this assumption have never even been considered. Therefore, a successful theory's anti-nihilist assumption must not be treated with the same respect that the reflected and tested components of the theory have earned. A theory's anti-nihilist assumption, while untested, might still be indispensable, though. The second step addresses the latter concern: a scientific theory's commitment to composites can be eliminated in a nihilism-friendly way (Rosen & Dorr, 2002; van Inwagen, 1990, ch. 11). Suppose, for instance, that a scientific theory contains the claim that there is something that is a molecule. This claim can be replaced by a nihilism-friendly counterpart that employs a plural quantifier and a plural predicate: there are some things that are arranged molecule-wise – or there are some things that collectively instantiate the property of being a molecule. These considerations suggest that our default position should be to treat a scientific theory's mereological assumptions as no more than convenient imports from ordinary thought and talk.

Assuming that the mere occurrence of composite-talk in successful scientific theories does not provide a good reason for opposing mereological nihilism, are there any substantive scientific considerations in favour of the existence of composites? An issue receiving increasing attention is whether the phenomenon of entanglement in quantum mechanics supports anti-nihilism. Let us have a brief look at one line of reasoning from entanglement to composites.

---

[63] Sider, 2013, sect. 5, adopts the second view. See Bostrom, 2003, for positive evidence in favour of the simulation-possibility.

[64] For further discussion, see Hofweber, 2016, ch. 7; Korman, 2015; Sattig, 2017.

Consider the following scenario (Einstein et al., 1935). An excited hydrogen molecule with spin zero decays into a pair of hydrogen atoms, *a* and *b*, whose spin is then measured. Prior to measurement, there are two possible outcomes of the measurement of *a* and *b*, respectively – namely, *a* is spin-up, *a* is spin-down, *b* is spin-up, and *b* is spin-down – which are equally likely to obtain. However, not all possible combinations of spin-states of *a* and *b* are equally likely. While the possible state of *a*'s being spin-up and *b*'s being spin-down, and the possible state of *b*'s being spin-up and *a*'s being spin-down each obtain with probability 0.5, the possible state of *a*'s being spin-up and *b*'s being spin-up and the possible state of *a*'s being spin-down and *b*'s being spin-down each obtain with probability 0. In fewer words, *a* and *b* are in a *superposition* of the combined state of *a*'s being spin-up and *b*'s being spin-down, and the combined state of *a*'s being spin-down and *b*'s being spin-up. This *anti-correlation* of *a*'s spin-state and *b*'s spin-state is a case of *entanglement*, which is illustrated in Figure 18 (where '*p*' stands for probability).

As a consequence of the entanglement of *a* and *b*, a measurement of *a* as being spin-up makes it certain that *b* is spin-down, and a measurement of *a* as being spin-down makes it certain that *b* is spin-up. And this is the case, irrespective of the spatial distance between *a* and *b* at the time of measurement. Such behaviour is baffling and cries out for an explanation. Where does the anti-correlation of *a*'s and *b*'s spin-states come from? What is its source?

The instinctive reaction of most is to seek a *causal explanation*. But it is implausible to hold that the measure result on *a* causes *b* to go into the opposite state or vice versa. This *non-locality* would require causation to be instantaneous. Instantaneous causation, however, stands in conflict with relativity theory, since it would require an interaction at a speed faster than the speed of light. Further, it would be implausible to hold that *a*'s and *b*'s spin are anti-correlated because *a*'s and *b*'s spin-states have the decay of the

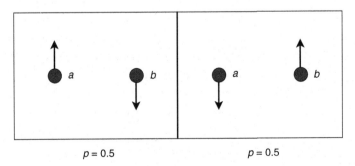

$p = 0.5$ $p = 0.5$

Figure 18 A case of entanglement

excited hydrogen molecule as their *common cause*. For reasons that we cannot go into here, this common-cause explanation is inconsistent with well-confirmed quantum statistics.

An alternative to giving a causal explanation is to postulate a fundamental relation of entanglement, which is expected to hold between a's and b's spin-states. The intrinsic states of a and b, respectively, do not explain their anti-correlation. Information about spatial relations between a and b, together with their spin-states, do not yield an explanation either. So one might see the need to add a new fundamental relation, the holding of which explains the anti-correlation in spin between a and b (Teller, 1986). This may well be the correct move, in the end. But in some sense it leaves the mystery of the co-variation of a's spin and b's spin unsolved. Expectations of what an adequate explanation should achieve might differ. But it would undoubtedly clear the fog to be able to show that a's spin-state and b's spin-state each have the same source. The fundamental-relation explanation does not, unfortunately, have that shape. For its strategy is to postulate a new external relation between a's and b's spin-states, which, intuitively speaking, treats these states as a given rather than telling us where they come from. And while a common-cause explanation would tell us where the two states come from, this style of explanation is not available here.

There is a further route: a *common-ground explanation* (Ismael & Schaffer, 2020).[65] Let us assume that, following the decay of our hydrogen molecule, a and b are parts of a composite two-particle system $a + b$. This composite has the total spin zero, and it is in a superposition of the combined state of a's being spin-up and b's being spin-down, and the combined state of a's being spin-down and b's being spin-up. As pointed out earlier, the intrinsic states of a and b, together with their spatial relations, do not explain this spin anti-correlation. Given the composite system, however, there is room to explore the idea that the anti-correlation is explained by the fact that $a + b$ is spin zero. The key thought is that the spin-state of $a + b$ is more fundamental than the spin-state of a and the spin-state of b. Moreover, the spin-state of a derives from, or is grounded in, the spin-state of $a + b$; the former is an aspect of, or an abstraction from, the latter. Analogously for the spin-state of b. Thus, the spin-states of a and b have the same source. Since this is a non-causal source, we have here the plan (though not yet the details) for a common-ground explanation. And since the intended explanation runs from the whole to its parts, it is committed to the existence of

---

[65] Compare the perspectival account of relativistic shapes discussed in Section 2.3. This is another instance of a common-ground explanation. See also Section 4.3.

a whole that has *a* and *b* as parts, which is incompatible with mereological nihilism.

Is this top-down schema of a common-ground explanation really committed to the existence of a composite of *a* and *b*? One might contemplate the following nihilism-friendly variant of the proposed schema: the spin-state of *a* and the spin-state of *b* both derive from the fact that *a* and *b* collectively instantiate the property of having spin zero (cf. Bohn, 2012, pp. 218–19; Brenner, 2018, p. 667). Since collective instantiation of a property by a plurality does not require the plurality to compose a whole, this variant of the schema incurs no anti-nihilist commitment. But what does collective property-instantiation by a plurality of things amount to? Consider two examples. First, some *x*s collectively instantiate the property of being spherical. This is a case of derivative instantiation: the *x*s collectively instantiate this shape-property, because the property consists in a pattern of spatial relations in which the *x*s stand to each other. Second, *x* and *y* collectively instantiate the property of having mass *m*, for some *m*. This is a further case of derivative instantiation: *x* and *y* collectively instantiate the property of having mass *m*, because *x* has mass n_1, *y* has mass n_2, and $n_1 + n_2 = m$. If all collective property-instantiation by a plurality derives from the standard instantiation of properties and/or relations by the individual members of the plurality – as seems plausible – then *a*'s and *b*'s collective instantiation of the property of being spin zero derives from properties and/or relations of *a* and *b*. But properties and relations of *a* and *b* are insufficient to explain their spin anti-correlation (assuming that there is no fundamental relation of entanglement). Hence, the proposed nihilism-friendly variant of the common-ground explanation may well turn out to be a red herring.

To conclude this brief discussion, if the version of the common-ground explanation presupposing the existence of a composite of *a* and *b* is the most illuminating explanation of *a*'s and *b*'s spin anti-correlation, then quantum entanglement provides support against mereological nihilism.[66]

4.2 Ontological Realism and Anti-Realism

A philosophical existence claim purports to describe a fact of existence. Different *ontological* positions express different views of which existence facts obtain. Different *metaontological* positions express different views of the nature of existence facts. The aim of this section is to review a range of metaontological positions and to apply them to the familiar ontological positions about the existence of composite material objects, namely, mereological restrictivism, universalism, and nihilism.

---

[66] For further discussion, see Brenner, 2018; Calosi, 2014; Calosi & Morganti, 2016, 2018.

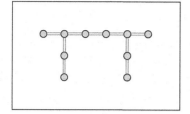 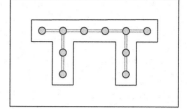

Figure 19 Standard ontological realism

According to *ontological realism*, philosophical existence claims all employ the same primitive notion of absolute existence. Existence is primitive when it cannot be analysed in existence-free terms.[67] *Standard* ontological realists also hold that the facts of primitive existence are determinate. There is no indeterminacy regarding which facts of primitive existence obtain. Further, standard ontological realists hold that the facts of existence are unitary. They are all of the same kind. (More on determinacy and unity shortly.)

How do standard ontological realists view the various ontological positions on the existence of composite material objects? According to them, mereological restrictivism, universalism, and nihilism compete for the correct account of the facts of primitive existence about composite material objects. Consider a very simple scenario that contains particles arranged tablewise. According to mereological nihilism, this scenario contains only the particles and no table. According to the other ontological positions, the scenario contains a table as well as the particles. The debate as construed by standard ontological realists is illustrated in Figure 19, where different boxes depict different views of the primitive existence of composite material objects. This is how the debate about composition and existence has been treated in previous sections.

Standard ontological realism has metaontological alternatives that yield construals of the ontological debate about composition and existence, which are quite different from the standard realist construal. I shall have a brief look at three alternatives. These views will not be discussed critically. My aim here is just to give an overview of some options. According to the first alternative, there are still facts of primitive existence. This makes the view a form of ontological realism. Moreover, there is only one kind of primitive-existence fact, as on standard ontological realism. However, some primitive-existence facts obtain indeterminately. Given that existence is a primitive notion, and hence does not

---

[67]   A fact of primitive existence need not be a fundamental fact. Many realists hold, for instance, that while it is a fact of primitive existence that tables exist, this fact is not fundamental, since it is grounded in facts about the parts of tables (see Section 1.2).

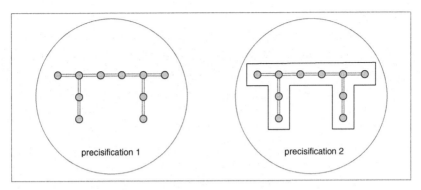

Figure 20 Ontological indeterminacy

permit different interpretations, this is a form of metaphysical indeterminacy, of representation-independent indeterminacy in the world.[68] Owing to this indeterminacy, we have here a variant of *non-standard* ontological realism.

When the ontological positions on composition and existence are conceived of from the point of view of this metaontological position, our toy scenario might be construed as one in which it is metaphysically indeterminate whether there are only particles arranged tablewise or whether there is a table in addition to the particles. Intuitively, there is one precisification of the scenario that makes the mereologial nihilist's description true, and there is another precisification that makes the description of the restrictivist and the universalist true. If one thinks of different precisifications of reality as different actual worlds (as I did in Section 3.3), then each of the ontological descriptions holds indeterminately because each is true in some but not all actual worlds.[69] The different precisifications of our scenario are illustrated in Figure 20 by means of two circles.

According to the second alternative, there are facts of primitive existence and these all obtain determinately, but they are not unitary facts, since there are different kinds of primitive property of existence, or different kinds of worldly existence-structure, different ways of being. To the different primitive existence-properties – the different basic ways of being – correspond different primitive notions of existence – or, more formally, different existential quantifiers – in terms of which existence claims in ontology may be formulated. This metaontological position is known as *ontological pluralism* (McDaniel, 2017; Turner, 2010). It is a further variant of non-standard ontological realism.

---

[68] Compare the indeterminacy of existence invoked in the context of the indeterminacy objection to restrictivism in Section 1.2.2.

[69] As pointed out before, the many-worlds gloss on metaphysical indeterminacy may be adopted while holding that metaphysical indeterminacy is itself primitive.

When applied to the ontological positions on composition and existence, ontological pluralism permits the following construal of our scenario. The particles arranged tablewise have the property of existence$_1$, but no table composed of these particles exists$_1$. However, a table does have the property of existence$_2$, and so do the particles arranged tablewise. In short, there are different, overlapping primitive domains of things. This construal of the ontological positions on composition are illustrated in Figure 20 when the two circles are interpreted as indicating that different primitive properties of existence, namely, existence$_1$ and existence$_2$, are in play. Notice that on this metaontological construal of the debate on composition, the different positions are compatible.[70]

According to the third alternative, there is no primitive existence. The only existence facts are facts of derivative existence. This metaontological position is known as *ontological nihilism* (to be distinguished from mereological nihilism; see Turner, 2011). Since the assumption of primitive existence defines ontological realism, ontological nihilism should be classified as a form of *ontological anti-realism*.

In order to grasp the radicalness of this approach, consider the following question. If reality is to be described as it is fundamentally, how is reality to be described by ontological nihilists? According to the latter, there are no fundamental facts of existence. For a fundamental fact of existence would have to be a fact of primitive existence, since a fact of derivative existence can be explained in other terms, and hence is non-fundamental. If reality contains objects, properties, or facts, these are all things that have existence – they are, more formally, all things in the domain of the absolutely unrestricted existential quantifier. Since there are no fundamental facts of existence, objects, properties, and facts are not denizens of fundamental reality. What, then, is the shape of fundamental reality? Consider the realist's fundamental truth that *a* is a particle. For the ontological nihilist neither particle *a* nor the property of being a particle exist fundamentally. What fundamental truth might the nihilist offer instead? One response is to offer fundamental descriptions of reality by statements that do not refer to objects, nor to any other things. As a first approximation, the nihilist might hold that, fundamentally, *it is particling* – by analogy with the ordinary, subject-less truth that it is snowing. Similarly, it might be asked what the nihilist proposes in place of the realist's fundamental

---

[70] Ontological pluralism has received comparatively little attention in contemporary metaphysics so far. And where it is discussed, different ways of being are taken to delineate different ontological categories, such as the categories of abstracta and of concreta, rather than different domains of material objects according to different views on composition. Nevertheless, it is useful to include the pluralist view of the composition debate in this line-up.

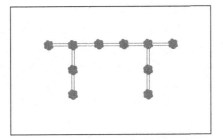

Figure 21 Ontological nihilism

truth that particles $a_1 \ldots a_n$ are arranged tablewise. Extending the suggestion mentioned earlier, the nihilist might hold that, fundamentally, *it is particling tablewise*.[71] Figure 21 is an attempt at illustrating the latter object-less truth.

While the previous three construals of the different ontological views on composition and existence recognize objects in their lowest-level description of our toy scenario, the nihilist outlook gives a fundamental description without reference to objects: it is particling tablewise. How, then, should the nihilist construe the different existence claims made by mereological nihilists, restrictivists, and universalists? If these claims are understood as purporting to describe facts of the *primitive* existence of certain material objects, then nihilists, restrictivists, and universalists all miss their target since there simply are no facts of primitive existence. A more inclusive option is to understand these existence claims as describing facts of the *derivative* existence of certain material objects. Furthermore, mereological nihilists and their opponents may be understood as describing derivative existence facts of different kinds, all of which are grounded in the same fundamental object-less truths.

Here is a rough implementation of this approach. Suppose that the correct fundamental description of our sample scenario is that it is particling tablewise. Somewhat more precisely, it is particling in one region, it is particling in another region, and so on. Further, it is particling tablewise across a plurality of regions.[72] Now say that there are two kinds of fact of derivative existence: existence$_1$ facts and existence$_2$ facts. They all derive from fundamental object-less truths by different grounding principles. First, existence$_1$. That it is particling in a given point-region grounds the fact that a particle exists$_1$, which is located in that region. Assuming that only atomic qualitative

---

[71] For rigorous formulations in terms of the language of predicate functorese, see Turner, 2011. See also O'Leary-Hawthorne & Cortens, 1995.

[72] For ease of exposition, let us help ourselves to talk of regions and moments, which are, strictly speaking, not permitted by ontological nihilism, since they are things.

truths, such as that it is particling in a certain point-region, give rise to facts of existence$_1$, the complete fundamental description of our scenario – that it is particling tablewise across a plurality of regions – explains that no table exists$_1$. Second, existence$_2$. That it is particling in a given region grounds the fact that a particle exists$_2$, which is located in that region. In addition, that it is particling tablewise across a plurality of regions also grounds the fact that a table exists$_2$, which is located at the sum of the atomic facts' locations. Therefore, a table exists$_2$. By these assumptions, the fundamental truths concerning particling in our scenario ground both the nihilist description, understood as concerning existence$_1$, and the restrictivist description, understood as concerning existence$_2$: no table exists$_1$ but a table does exist$_2$, while particles arranged tablewise both exist$_1$ and exist$_2$. To sum up, according to the version of ontological nihilism under consideration, the mereological descriptions of our toy scenario are about different kinds of fact of derivative existence. And since the latter derive from the same fundamental facts by independent grounding principles, the descriptions are compatible. (I shall return to this construal of the ontological debate about composition at the end of Section 4.3.)

4.3 Deflationism about the Ontology of Objects

Deflationism about a debate in ontology is the view that the debate is metaphysically superficial. Since deflationism about a given debate does not aim for a general account of the nature of existence facts, but rather targets a specific first-order debate, deflationism is not meant to be a metaontological position of the sort reviewed in Section 4.2.

Deflationism about the debate on composition and existence in the domain of material objects – henceforth simply 'the debate' – has been defended by a number of metaphysicians.[73] It is also a rather popular view among philosophers working outside of metaphysics and among undergraduate students and non-philosophers, at least as they encounter the debate for the first time. Deflationists about the debate agree that nothing of great philosophical significance is at stake in it. There is, according to them, no need to get worked up about the issue in the seminar room, since the debate does not belong in the seminar room in the first place.

Why do they believe this? To begin with, contemporary deflationists do not believe this just because the different positions on composition and existence are empirically indistinguishable – that is, because the debate cannot be decided

---

[73] Hilary Putnam and Eli Hirsch are leading proponents. Hirsch is also a deflationist about the persistence debate. I shall focus on composition here. See Hirsch, 2002a, 2002b, 2005; Putnam, 1987, 2004. See Thomasson, 2007, for a different kind of ontological deflationism.

by experience or experiment. Present-day deflationists are not verificationists. They are well aware that science, especially theoretical physics, hosts a number of substantive debates whose positions offer competing accounts of matters that are unobservable, while agreeing on matters that are observable. These debates cannot be decided by experiment, either.[74]

A popular overture to ontological deflationism is this claim: the debate is all about the use of language. The debate is thought to be merely verbal, in that the debaters attach different meanings to the expressions 'existence' and 'there is' – or, more formally, to the existential quantifier '∃'. For each position in the debate, there is a meaning of 'existence', relative to which the position is correct. Moreover, all the meanings of 'existence' in use in the debate are on a par. *Parity* is a central component in deflationism. How is this notion to be understood? Since language is conventional, it is trivial that 'existence' can be used with many different meanings. The deflationist's parity of meanings of a given expression must amount to more than the obvious fact that they are all possible meanings of the expression. There must be more in common among these meanings, in order for them to be on a par, in the relevant sense.[75]

The following image is often employed by deflationists, in order to convey an initial sense of the intended parity. Consider, again, the simple scenario of a plurality of particles arranged tablewise. According to the mereological nihilist, the particles $exist_1$ but no table $exists_1$, whereas according to certain mereological restrictivists, a table $exists_2$ and so do the particles. These descriptions employ different concepts of existence. Now, the two descriptions are on a par, in virtue of 'cutting' the same 'piece of reality' into objects in different, equally appropriate ways, just as the same piece of dough can be cut into different sets of cookies in different, equally appropriate ways. Different concepts of existence are different object-making tools by which an 'amorphous reality' is 'carved' into various sets of objects.[76] This image suggests that the deflationist's parity of different meanings of 'existence' does not just concern the use of language, and that it also concerns these meanings' relationship to reality. More work is required, though, in order to turn the cookie-cutter image into a philosophical thesis apt for theoretical processing.

The following clarification echoes how some ontological deflationists think about parity. As applied to our example, the thought is that the mereological nihilist's statement that tablewise arranged particles $exist_1$ but no table $exists_1$, and the mereological restrictivist's statement that a table $exists_2$ in addition to tablewise arranged particles, are *necessarily equivalent* – that they

---

[74] See Hawthorne, 2009, p. 214, for examples.   [75] See Sider, 2011, pp. 67–70, on parity.
[76] See Eklund, 2008, for references.

are true in the same metaphysically possible worlds.[77] The two statements describe the same set of possibilities – the same *intension* – by means of different concepts of existence. By considering the set of possible worlds described by a statement, we hone in on the portion of reality described by the statement, in virtue of varying all the aspects of a world that are not required for the statement's truth. The hazy idea that the two descriptions carve the same portion of amorphous reality into objects in different ways can then be clarified by saying that the two statements describe the same set of worlds. In order to leave some room for different views about whether necessary equivalence is sufficient for parity, let us just focus on the weaker thesis that it is required for parity. In the remainder of this section, I shall look at two challenges for this deflationist thesis.[78]

The first challenge is that while different voices in the debate make claims that, by deflationist lights, describe the same portion of reality, these claims are not true in the same set of possible worlds. Here is an example (due to Hawthorne, 2009, p. 221). Consider the following scenario, as described by a typical mereological restrictivist. At moment t_1, a plurality of particles, the xs, compose a table, A, and at moment t_2, the same xs compose a non-identical table, B. Mereological nihilists deny that there are any tables in this scenario. They hold that the xs exist at t_1 and at t_2, while they do not compose any table at any moment. According to the deflationist, the restrictivist description and the nihilist description capture the same portion of reality in different ways, and hence are on a par. By the modal account of parity, the two descriptions are true in the same set of metaphysically possible worlds. This claim, however, is false. Let the scenario above obtain in world w_1. The restrictivist distinguishes w_1 from a world, w_2, in which the xs compose a table at t_1 and a non-identical table at t_2, but in which the order of the tables is switched: the xs compose B at t_1, while composing A at t_2, as illustrated in Figure 22. The differences between w_1 and w_2 are *haecceitistic* differences. They are differences concerning *which* table exists at t_1 and *which* exists at t_2. While the restrictivist description at the outset is true at w_1, it is false at w_2. The nihilist description, by contrast, is true at w_1 and at w_2, since for the nihilist w_2 just is w_1. That is, the restrictivist distinguishes haecceitistic possibilities for tables, to which the nihilist is

---

[77] I shall assume with Hirsch and other deflationists that statements about necessity and possible worlds are metaphysically deep statements. Few contemporary metaphysicians are deflationists about modality. Though see Sider, 2011, ch. 12.

[78] Notice that this intensional account of parity says nothing about whether the existence concepts involved are primitive. Recall from Section 4.2 that ontological pluralists recognize a plurality of existence concepts that can be said to be on a par because they are all primitive. The ontological pluralist's parity thesis is to be distinguished from the deflationist's. The latter is meant to be much less metaphysically heavyweight than the former.

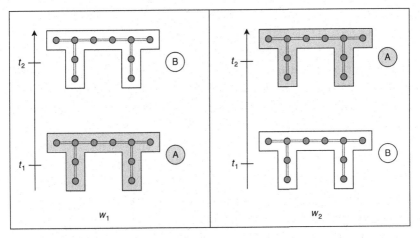

Figure 22 Haecceitistic differences

blind. Hence, the initial restrictivist description and the nihilist description do not capture the same portion of reality. They are not on a par.[79]

The second challenge is that the necessary equivalence that establishes parity among the various positions in the debate requires an explanation. Let us assume that the mereological nihilist's statement that tablewise arranged particles exist$_1$ but no table exists$_1$, and the mereological restrictivist's statement that a table exists$_2$ in addition to the tablewise arranged particles, is true in the same metaphysically possible worlds. Now why is that so? An equivalence of distinct contingent descriptions across all possible worlds is a super strong equivalence. It would be astonishing if it held just like that, without there being any explanation for why it holds. So, what is the source of this necessary equivalence?[80,81]

A natural explanation is to say that the nihilist fact that tablewise arranged particles exist$_1$ but no table exists$_1$, and the restrictivist fact that a table exists$_2$ as well as tablewise arranged particles, derive from the same fundamental facts. The idea is simple. Any fundamental fact that grounds the nihilist fact in any possible world also grounds the restrictivist fact, and vice versa. If the nihilist fact and the restrictivist fact have a common ground in any world – leaving room for their common ground to vary from world to world – then it is no

---

[79] Compare the collapse problem of Section 2.2.

[80] Compare the explanatory challenge presented by entanglement in Section 4.1.

[81] It would be implausible to explain the necessary equivalence by sameness of meaning. The few who hold that the two descriptions have the same meaning believe that sameness of meaning results from the descriptions' necessary equivalence, not the other way around.

surprise that in each world in which one shows up, the other shows up too, and vice versa.

In Section 4.2, we encountered a range of metaontological frameworks and applied them to the debate on composition and existence. This metaontological menu becomes relevant as we search for a common ground of the nihilist's existence$_1$ facts and the restrictivist's existence$_2$ facts. On the assumption of standard ontological realism with its determinate and unitary facts of primitive existence, a distinction between different kinds of existence fact is highly unnatural. What about the alternative metaontological pictures? Setting aside, for simplicity, ontological indeterminacy and ontological pluralism, I shall focus on why ontological nihilism opens up a promising implementation of the aforementioned explanatory scheme.

According to ontological nihilism, nothing exists fundamentally. So the lowest-level truths are not about existence and not about objects. Suppose with the ontological nihilist that the correct fundamental description of our toy scenario is that it is particling tablewise across a plurality of spatial regions. Recall, furthermore, that there are two kinds of fact of derivative existence. Facts of existence$_1$ and facts of existence$_2$ derive from fundamental object-less truths by different, independent grounding principles. Roughly, that it is particling in a given point-region grounds the fact that a particle exists$_1$ that is located in that region. Assuming that only atomic qualitative truths, such as that it is particling in a certain point-region, give rise to facts of existence$_1$, the complete fundamental description of our scenario grounds that no table exists$_1$. Furthermore, that it is particling in a given region grounds the fact that a particle exists$_2$, which is located in that region. In addition, that it is particling tablewise across a plurality of regions also grounds the fact that a table exists$_2$, which is located at the sum of the atomic facts' locations. Therefore, a table exists$_2$. The fundamental truths concerning particling in our scenario thus ground both the nihilist description and the restrictivist description. Assuming that the nihilist's existence$_1$ facts and the restrictivist's existence$_2$ facts are generated in the same way – by the same grounding principles, respectively – in each world in which they obtain, the grounds of the existence$_1$ facts are, in each world, also grounds of the existence$_2$ facts, and vice versa. Hence, the existence facts co-obtain necessarily.

Notice that this ontological-nihilist explanation of the targeted necessary equivalence is not just one among equal candidates. For it is quite plausible that the common ground of the two descriptions must be an object-less truth. In order to explain the necessary co-obtainment of our existence$_1$ fact and our existence$_2$ fact, we seek a common ground that is neutral with respect to existence$_1$ facts and existence$_2$ facts. Since every object-involving fact will be a fact that either presupposes existence$_1$ or existence$_2$ – each object belongs to the domain of existents$_1$ or to the domain of existents$_2$ – a neutral ground will be object-neutral. And the framework of ontological nihilism promises just that.

By this route, we reach an anti-realist explanation of the necessary equivalence of the nihilist and restrictivist descriptions, which advances upon the modal account of parity and offers a more thorough understanding of this notion. We can now say that the rival positions are on a par, in virtue of being about derivative object facts – existence$_1$ facts and existence$_2$ facts, respectively – that are grounded in the same object-less fundamental truths. The initial, hazy picture of an amorphous portion of reality that is carved into objects in different ways thus receives a respectable sharpening within the framework of ontological nihilism. Reality is amorphous, doughlike, with respect to objects, in virtue of being ultimately object-neutral. Different ontologies of objects furnish a fundamentally object-less reality with objects in different ways, by formulating different principles governing the grounding of existence facts.

Ontological nihilism looks like a perfect match for the deflationists' cookie-cutter image. The path of clarifying this image naturally leads to ontological nihilism. This metaontological position, however, ultimately betrays the spirit of deflationism. Recall that deflationists about the debate agree that nothing of great philosophical significance is at stake in it. But if deflationism needs ontological nihilism to explain parity, then the deflationist is forced to enter a debate of significant philosophical interest, namely, the metaphysically deep debate between ontological realism and anti-realism, where different heavy-weight positions compete against each other. Notice that this betrayal of the deflationist spirit does not depend on taking the ontological-nihilist route. It occurs as soon as the deflationist turns to the metaontological buffet of heavy-weight views on which facts or truths are fundamental, as she seeks a satisfactory account of the parity of different ontological views on material objects. If deflationists make an honest effort of advancing beyond pictures, then substantive discussions in the seminar room are unavoidable.[82]

---

[82] For further discussion, see Sider, 2011, chs. 4 and 9.

References

Akiba, K. 2000: 'Vagueness as a Modality', *Philosophical Quarterly*, 50: 359–70.

Akiba, K. & Abasnezhad, A. (eds.) 2014: *Vague Objects and Vague Identity: New Essays on Ontoc Vagueness*. Berlin: Springer.

Armstrong, D. M. 1980: 'Identity through Time', in P. van Inwagen (ed.), *Time and Cause: Essays Presented to Richard Taylor*, Dordrecht: D. Reidel, pp. 67–78.

Baker, L. R. 2007: *The Metaphysics of Everyday Life: An Essay in Practical Realism*. Cambridge: Cambridge University Press.

Baker, L. R. 2000: *Persons and Bodies: A Constitution View*. Cambridge: Cambridge University Press.

Balashov, Y. 2010: *Persistence and Spacetime*. Oxford: Oxford University Press.

Barnes, E. & Williams, J. R. G. 2011: 'A Theory of Metaphysical Indeterminacy', *Oxford Studies in Metaphysics*, 6: 103–48.

Bennett, K. 2017: *Making Things Up*. Oxford: Oxford University Press.

Bennett, K. 2013: 'Having a Part Twice Over', *Australasian Journal of Philosophy*, 91: 83–103.

Bennett, K. 2004: 'Spatio-Temporal Coincidence and the Grounding Problem', *Philosophical Studies*, 118: 339–71.

Bohn, E. D. 2012: 'Monism, Emergence, and Plural Logic', *Erkenntnis*, 76: 211–23.

Bostrom, N. 2003: 'Are You Living in a Computer Simulation?', *Philosophical Quarterly*, 53: 243–55.

Brenner, A. 2018: 'Science and the Special Composition Question', *Synthese*, 195: 657–78.

Burke, X. 1994: 'Preserving the Principle of One Object to a Place: A Novel Account of the Relations among Objects, Sorts, Sortals, and Persistence Conditions', *Philosophy and Phenomenological Research*, 54: 591–624.

Butterfield, J. 2005: 'On the Persistence of Particles', *Foundations of Physics*, 35: 233–69.

Calosi, C. 2014: 'Quantum Mechanics and Priority Monism', *Synthese*, 191: 915–28.

Calosi, C. & Costa, D. 2015: 'Multilocation, Fusion and Confusions', *Philosophia*, 43: 25–33.

Calosi, C. & Morganti, M. 2021: 'Interpreting Quantum Entanglement: Steps towards Coherentist Quantum Mechanics', *British Journal for the Philosophy of Science*, 72: 865–91.

Calosi, C. & Morganti, M. 2016: 'Humean Supervenience, Composition as Identity and Quantum Wholes', *Erkenntnis*, 81: 1173–94.

Carmichael, C. 2015: 'Toward a Commonsense Answer to the Special Composition Question', *Australasian Journal of Philosophy*, 93: 475–90.

Costa, D. 2017: 'The Transcendentist Theory of Persistence', *Journal of Philosophy*, 114: 57–75.

Cotnoir, A. J. & Baxter, D. L. M. (eds.) 2014: *Composition as Identity*. Oxford: Oxford University Press.

Cotnoir, A. J. & Varzi, A. C. 2021: *Mereology*. Oxford: Oxford University Press.

deRosset, L. 2011: 'What Is the Grounding Problem?', *Philosophical Studies*, 156: 173–97.

Donnelly, M. 2010: 'Parthood and Multi-location', *Oxford Studies in Metaphysics*, 5: 203–43.

Eagle, A. 2016: 'Location and Perdurance', *Oxford Studies in Metaphysics*, 5: 53–94.

Eddon, M. 2010: 'Three Arguments from Temporary Intrinsics', *Philosophy and Phenomenological Research*, 81: 605–17.

Einstein, A., Podolsky, B., & Rosen, N. 1935: 'Can Quantum-Mechanical Descriptions of Reality Be Considered Complete?', *Physical Review*, 47: 777–80.

Eklund, M. 2008: 'The Picture of Reality as an Amorphous Lump', in T. Sider, J. Hawthorne, & D. W. Zimmerman (eds.), *Contemporary Debates in Metaphysics*, Blackwell, pp. 382–96.

Evnine, S. J. 2016: *Making Objects and Events: A Hylomorphic Theory of Artifacts, Actions, and Organisms*. Oxford: Oxford University Press.

Fine, K. 2010: 'Towards a Theory of Part', *Journal of Philosophy*, 107: 559–89.

Fine, K. 2008: 'Coincidence and Form', *Proceedings of the Aristotelian Society*, 82: 101–18.

Fine, K. 2003: 'The Non-identity of a Material Thing and Its Matter', *Mind*, 112: 195–234.

Fine, K. 2000: 'A Counter-example to Locke's Thesis', *Monist*, 83: 357–61.

Fine, K. 1999: 'Things and Their Parts', *Midwest Studies in Philosophy*, 23: 61–74.

Fine, K. 1975: 'Vagueness, Truth and Logic', *Synthese*, 30: 265–300.

Gallois, A. 2003: *Occasions of Identity*. Oxford: Oxford University Press.

Geach, P. 1980: *Reference and Generality*. Ithaca, NY: Cornell University Press.

Gibbard, A. 1975: 'Contingent Identity', *Journal of Philosophical Logic*, 4: 187–221.

Gibson, I. & Pooley, O. 2006: 'Relativistic Persistence', *Philosophical Perspectives*, 20: 157–98.

Gilmore, C. 2008: 'Persistence and Location in Relativistic Spacetime', *Philosophy Compass*, 3/6: 1224–54.

Gilmore, C. 2006: 'Where in the Relativistic World Are We?', *Philosophical Perspectives*, 20: 199–236.

Haslanger, S. 1989: 'Persistence, Change, and Explanation', *Philosophical Studies*, 56: 1–18.

Hawley, K. 2002: 'Vagueness and Existence', *Proceedings of the Aristotelian Society*, 102: 125–40.

Hawley, K. 2001: *How Things Persist*. Oxford: Oxford University Press.

Hawthorne, J. 2009: 'Superficialism in Ontology', in D. Manley, D. J. Chalmers, & R. Wasserman (eds.), *Metametaphysics: New Essays on the Foundations of Ontology*, Oxford University Press, pp. 213–30.

Hawthorne, J. 2006: *Metaphysical Essays*. Oxford: Oxford University Press.

Heller, M. 1991: *The Ontology of Physical Objects: Four-Dimensional Hunks of Matter*. New York: Cambridge University Press.

Hestevold, H. S. 1981: 'Conjoining', *Philosophy and Phenomenological Research*, 41: 371–85.

Hinchliff, M. 1996: 'The Puzzle of Change', *Philosophical Perspectives*, 10: 119–36.

Hirsch, E. 2005: 'Physical-Object Ontology, Verbal Disputes, and Common Sense', *Philosophy and Phenomenological Research*, 70: 67–97.

Hirsch, E. 2002a: 'Against Revisionary Ontology', *Philosophical Topics*, 30: 103–27.

Hirsch, E. 2002b: 'Quantifier Variance and Realism', *Philosophical Issues*, 12: 51–73.

Hofweber, T. 2016: *Ontology and the Ambitions of Metaphysics*. Oxford: Oxford University Press.

Hofweber, T. 2009: 'The Meta-problem of Change', *Noûs*, 43: 286–314.

Hofweber, T. & Velleman, J. D. 2010: 'How to Endure', *Philosophical Quarterly*, 61: 37–57.

Ismael, J. & Schaffer, J. 2020: 'Quantum Holism: Nonseparability as Common Ground', *Synthese*, 197: 4131–60.

Johnston, M. 1987: 'Human Beings', *Journal of Philosophy*, 84: 59–83.

Jubien, M. 2001: 'Thinking about Things', *Philosophical Perspectives*, 15: 1–15.

Korman, D. 2015: *Objects: Nothing Out of the Ordinary*. Oxford: Oxford University Press.

Korman, D. 2010: 'The Argument from Vagueness', *Philosophy Compass*, 5/10: 891–901.

Korman, D. 2008: 'Unrestricted Composition and Restricted Quantification', *Philosophical Studies*, 140: 319–34.

Korman, D. & Carmichael, C. 2017: 'What Do the Fol Think about Composition and Does It Matter?', in D. Rose (ed.), *Experimental Metaphysics*, Bloomsbury Academic, pp. 187–206.

Koslicki, K. 2018: *Form, Matter, Substance*. Oxford: Oxford University Press.

Koslicki, K. 2008: *The Structure of Objects*. Oxford: Oxford University Press.

Kovacs, D. M. 2020: 'Constitution and Dependence', *Journal of Philosophy*, 117: 150–77.

Langford, S. & Ramachandran, M. 2013: 'The Products of Fission, Fusion, and Teletransportation: An Occasional Identity Theorist's Perspective', *Australasian Journal of Philosophy*, 91: 105–17.

Lewis, D. 1999: 'Zimmerman and the Spinning Sphere', *Australasian Journal of Philosophy*, 77: 209–12.

Lewis, D. 1993: 'Many, But Almost One', in K. Campbell, J. Bacon, & L. Reinhardt (eds.), *Ontology, Causality, and Mind: Essays in Honour of D. M. Armstrong*, Cambridge University Press, pp. 23–38.

Lewis, D. 1988: 'Rearrangement of Particles: Reply to Lowe', *Analysis*, 48: 65–72.

Lewis, D. 1986: *On the Plurality of Worlds*. Oxford: Blackwell.

Lewis, D. 1983a: 'Survival and Identity', in his *Philosophical Papers*, Vol. 1, Oxford University Press, pp. 55–77.

Lewis, D. 1983b: 'Counterparts of Persons and Their Bodies', in his *Philosophical Papers*, Vol. 1, Oxford University Press, pp. 203–11.

Locke, J. 1690/1975: *An Essay Concerning Human Understanding*, ed. P. H. Nidditch. Oxford: Clarendon Press.

Markosian, N. 2008: 'Restricted Composition', in T. Sider, J. Hawthorne, & D. W. Zimmerman (eds.), *Contemporary Debates in Metaphysics*, Blackwell, pp. 341–63.

McDaniel, K. 2017: *The Fragmentation of Being*. Oxford: Oxford University Press.

McGee, V. & McLaughlin, B. 2000: 'The Lessons of the Many', *Philosophical Topics*, 28: 129–51.

McKenzie, K. & Muller, F. A. 2018: 'Bound States and the Special Composition Question', in M. Massimi, J.-W. Romejin, & G. Schurz (eds.), *EPSA 15 Selected Papers*, Springer, pp. 233–42.

McKinnon, N. 2002: 'Supervaluations and the Problem of the Many', *Philosophical Quartely*, 52: 320–39.

Merricks, T. 2001: *Objects and Persons*. New York: Oxford University Press.

Nozick, R. 1981: *Philosophical Explanations*. Oxford: Clarendon Press.

O'Leary-Hawthorne, J. & Cortens, A. 1995: 'Towards Ontological Nihilism', *Philosophical Studies*, 79: 143–65.

Parfit, D. 1984: *Reasons and Persons*. Oxford: Clarendon Press.

Parsons, J. 2007: 'Theories of Location', *Oxford Studies in Metaphysics*, 3: 201–32.

Parsons, T. 2000: *Indeterminate Identity*. Oxford: Oxford University Press.

Pooley, O. 2019: 'There is Invariant Four-Dimensional Stuff', unpublished manuscript, University of Oxford.

Putnam, H. 2004: *Ethics without Ontology*. Cambridge, MA: Harvard University Press.

Putnam, H. 1987: *The Many Faces of Realism*. La Salle: Open Court.

Rea, M. 2000: 'Constitution and Kind Membership', *Philosophical Studies*, 97: 169–93.

Rea, M. 1997: 'Supervenience and Co-Location', *American Philosophical Quarterly*, 34: 367–75.

Rose, D. & Schaffer, J. 2017: 'Folk Mereology is Teleological', *Noûs*, 51: 238–70.

Rosen, G. & Dorr, C. 2002: 'Composition as a Fiction', in R. Gale (ed.), *The Blackwell Compaion to Metaphysics*, Blackwell, pp. 151–74.

Saenz, N. B. 2015: 'A Grounding Solution to the Grounding Problem', *Philosophical Studies*, 172: 2193–214.

Sattig, T. 2019: 'Part, Slot, Ground: Foundations for Neo-Aristotelian Mereology', *Synthese*, 198: 2735–49.

Sattig, T. 2017: 'Metaphysical Ambitions in the Ontology of Objects', *Philosophy and Phenomenological Research*, 94: 481–87.

Sattig, T. 2015: *The Double Lives of Objects: An Essay in the Metaphysics of the Ordinary World*. Oxford: Oxford University Press.

Sattig, T. 2010: 'Compatibilism about Coincidence', *Philosophical Review*, 119: 273–313.

Sattig, T. 2006: *The Language and Reality of Time*. Oxford: Oxford University Press.

Schaffer, J. 2009: 'On What Grounds What', in D. Manley, D. J. Chalmers, & R. Wasserman (eds.), *Metametaphysics: New Essays on the Foundations of Ontology*, Oxford University Press, pp. 347–83.

Shoemaker, S. 1963: *Self-Knowledge and Self-Identity*. Ithaca, NY: Cornell University Press.

Sider, T. 2013: 'Against Parthood', *Oxford Studies in Metaphysics*, 8: 237–93.

Sider, T. 2011: *Writing the Book of the World*. Oxford: Oxford University Press.

Sider, T. 2001: *Four-Dimensionalism: Ontology of Persistence and Time*. Oxford: Oxford University Press.

Sutton, C. S. 2012: 'Colocated Objects, Tally-Ho: A Solution to the Grounding Problem', *Mind*, 121: 703–30.

Teller, P. 1986: 'Relational Holism and Quantum Mechanics', *British Journal for the Philosophy of Science*, 37: 71–81.

Thomasson, A. 2007: *Ordinary Objects*. Oxford: Oxford University Press.

Thomson, J. J. 1998: 'The Statue and the Clay', *Noûs*, 32: 149–73.

Turner, J. 2011: 'Ontological Nihilism', *Oxford Studies in Metaphysics*, 6: 3–54.

Turner, J. 2010: 'Ontological Pluralism', *Journal of Philosophy*, 107: 5–34.

Unger, P. 1980: 'The Problem of the Many', *Midwest Studies in Philosophy*, 5: 411–67.

Unger, P. 1979: 'There Are No Ordinary Things', *Synthese*, 41: 117–54.

van Inwagen, P. 1990: *Material Beings*. Ithaca, NY: Cornell University Press.

Wallace, M. 2011a: 'Composition as Identity: Part 1', *Philosophy Compass*, 6/11: 804–16.

Wallace, M. 2011b: 'Composition as Identity: Part 2', *Philosophy Compass*, 6/11: 817–27.

Wasserman, R. 2016: 'Theories of Persistence', *Philosophical Studies*, 173: 243–50.

Weatherson, B. 2016: 'The Problem of the Many', The Stanford Encyclopedia of Philosophy (Winter 2016 Edition), Edward N. Zalta (ed.), https://plato .stanford.edu/archives/win2016/entries/problem-of-many/.

Wiggins, D. 1967: *Identity and Spatio-Temporal Continuity*. Oxford: Blackwell.

Williams, B. A. O. 1956: 'Personal Identity and Individuation', *Proceedings of the Aristotelian Society*, 57: 229–52.

Zimmerman, D. 1999: 'One Really Big Liquid Sphere: Reply to Lewis', *Australasian Journal of Philosophy*, 77: 213–15.

Zimmerman, D. 1998: 'Temporal Parts and Supervenient Causation: The Incompatibility of Two Humean Doctrines', *Australasian Journal of Philosophy*, 76: 265–88.

Zimmerman, D. 1997: 'Immanent Causation', *Philosophical Perspectives*, 11: 433–71.

Zimmerman, D. 1995: 'Theories of Masses and Problems of Constitution', *Philosophical Review*, 104: 53–110.

Acknowledgement

For many helpful comments on previous drafts of this Element I am indebted to Claudius Berger, Claudio Calosi, Damiano Costa, Dan Korman, Tobias Wilsch, and two anonymous reviewers for CUP.

Cambridge Elements ☰

Metaphysics

Tuomas E. Tahko
University of Bristol

Tuomas E. Tahko is Professor of Metaphysics of Science at the University of Bristol, UK. Tahko specializes in contemporary analytic metaphysics, with an emphasis on methodological and epistemic issues: 'meta-metaphysics'. He also works at the interface of metaphysics and philosophy of science: 'metaphysics of science'. Tahko is the author of *Unity of Science* (CUP, 2021, *Elements in Philosophy of Science*), *An Introduction to Metametaphysics* (CUP, 2015) and editor of *Contemporary Aristotelian Metaphysics* (CUP, 2012).

About the Series
This highly accessible series of Elements provides brief but comprehensive introductions to the most central topics in metaphysics. Many of the Elements also go into considerable depth, so the series will appeal to both students and academics. Some Elements bridge the gaps between metaphysics, philosophy of science, and epistemology.

Cambridge Elements $\equiv$

Metaphysics

Elements in the Series